Library of Congress Cataloging-in-Publication Data

Names: Dobbs, Troy, 1967- author.
Title: The blessed life... : that no one really wants / written by Troy Dobbs.
Description: Minneapolis : TRISTAN Publishing, [2020] | Summary: "The
Blessed Life...That No One Really Wants, is written with the goal of
expanding and broadening our understanding of God's blessings. In the
book Pastor Troy Dobbs explores and explains the timeless message shared
by Jesus in the Sermon on the Mount"— Provided by publisher
Identifiers: LCCN 2019018151 | ISBN 9781939881205
Subjects: LCSH: Sermon on the Mount—Criticism, interpretation, etc.
Classification: LCC BT380.3 .D63 2019 | DDC 226.9/306—dc23
LC record available at https://lccn.loc.gov/2019018151

TRISTAN Publishing, Inc.
2355 Louisiana Avenue North
Golden Valley, MN 55427

Text copyright © 2020, Troy Dobbs
ISBN 978-1-939881-20-5
Printed in Canada
First Printing

THE BLESSED LIFE

that no one really wants

TROY DOBBS

TRISTAN PUBLISHING

MINNEAPOLIS

Table of Contents

Grateful to Cheri,

Delaney, Marlee, Drake, and Jax—

and to my Grace Church family.

~Troy

Introduction

I love the Bible, and I love Christ's Church. Fortunately, since
1994, I've been able to consistently preach and teach the Bible
and lead in a church. Thus, out of my own experience in the
church and my concern *for* the church, I have felt burdened
to build up the body of Christ by broadening and strengthen-
ing—biblically—how God's people understand the blessing
of God. In particular, I want to challenge the wildly popular
prosperity gospel (that God promises us all health and wealth)
by exploring a message of Jesus called the Beatitudes in the
Sermon on the Mount. From my own experience and through
careful study, I've come to the conclusion that the Beatitudes
are the Blessings of God . . . *no one really wants.*

CHAPTER 1

BLESSED ARE THE POOR IN SPIRIT

> Blessed are the poor in spirit,
> for theirs is the kingdom of heaven.
> MATTHEW 5:3

Today in Christian circles, a scandalous amount of warped teaching is floating around regarding prosperity and the "blessing" of God. The teaching is fundamentally flawed, biblically indefensible, and conspicuously one-sided.

It goes something like this (in your best big-booming, bass voice): "God is a God of blessing; God has a destiny of financial breakthrough for you!" The catch is that "blessing" is then appropriated through our worldly reward system as bling, rings, and more things. Under this criterion, the unsound teaching becomes a perpetual lesson in how to readjust and realign your life to tap in to those blessings. And, according to this false teaching, if, as a Christ-follower, you don't experience those type of blessings, it's nobody's fault but your own: it's either a lack of faith or a leanness in the sowing and reaping department.

As such, this deceptive teaching propagates an overly simplistic formula as it pertains to relating to God: just crack the

"God code," and God is duty-bound to bless. Obviously, God is *not* a problem to solve or a code to crack. Moreover, do we *really* believe we can manipulate God into releasing what is in his hand? And do we really believe that the only things in his hand are *things*?

The worst of this teaching is that it reduces the Christian experience to simply **getting** something from God. And our *getting* something **out of** God trumps our *loving* God with all of our heart, mind, soul, and strength and our *loving* our neighbors as ourselves as we know from Matthew 22:37–40. In addition, it eclipses our living all out for the glory of God, instead of ourselves (1 Corinthians 10:31).

To be fair, let me say something from the outset. I do believe the Bible teaches that God is a God of blessing and he does desire to bless his people (Genesis 12 and Acts 3:26). And I do believe God blesses his people materially, but not all the time—and not just materially!

Unfortunately, the pervading concept of *blessing* in religious America has been notoriously equated with the American Dream, instead of the gospel of Christ. Today *blessing* seems to mean something altogether different.

- Promotion, not Persecution
- Success, not Suffering

- Getting Invited, not Getting Insulted
- Bigger, not Smaller
- Health, not Pain
- More, not Less
- Now, not Later

Surprisingly, the silence is deafening in Christian circles when it comes to the categories introduced in the Beatitudes such as *persecution, suffering, insult, smaller, pain,* and *less* as actually being a part of the biblical equation of blessing, too! These are the blessings of God no one seems to talk much about—or recognize or even want—today. Therefore, the irony in all of this is that when we settle for a truncated definition of the word *blessing,* we are destined not for a life of blessing, but rather for a life of frustration, defeat, and misguided striving. I can personally attest to this experience. During the first decade of my own journey with Christ, I was in a perpetual state of spiritual exhaustion, trying to earn God's blessing, grace, and love. It was only after reading a book by Philip Yancey called *What's So Amazing About Grace?* that I began to learn to rest in Christ. In the book, he said this: "Grace means there is nothing I can do to make God love me more, and nothing I can do to make God love me less. It means that I, even I who deserve the opposite, am invited to take my place at the table in God's family. By instinct I feel I must *do something* in order to be accepted. Grace sounds a startling note of contradiction, of liberation, and every day I must pray anew for the ability to hear its message."[1] I'll never forget how those words freed me from striving for his love, blessing, and grace—by simply receiving them. That's a good word, isn't it? Every day we need to pray for the ability to hear the message of grace again. Additionally—and I think most importantly—if our Christian experience is consumed only with the pursuit of God's blessings, then it comes at the high cost of missing the greatest blessing of all—God himself (Genesis 15:1).

I do realize that a casual reading of the Beatitudes might leave you scratching your head in confusion. I get it. At first glance, they don't seem like great life strategies to employ in order to be successful, happy, and blessed. My guess is that we'd all be clamoring for them if they were more American Dream-esque.

- Blessed are **the rich in cash**, for theirs is a fulfilled life.
- Blessed are **those who party all the time**, for they will be entertained.
- Blessed are **the strong and dominant**, for they will be in control.
- Blessed are **those who are full and in need of nothing**, for they will be satisfied.

- Blessed are **the cutthroat**, for they will always win.
- Blessed are **the pleasure seekers**, for they shall be thrilled.
- Blessed are **those who stay in their own lanes and do their own things**, for they will avoid confrontation.
- Blessed are **the untouched and unharmed**, for theirs is the life of ease.

And so, we have to ask ourselves some important questions.

- How is **being poor in spirit** a blessing?
- How does **mourning** not leave you depressed?
- How does **being meek** actually get you ahead in life?
- How is **hungering and thirsting for righteousness** relevant in the twenty-first century, anyway?

Well, don't forget that the Beatitudes are Jesus' insights into the blessed life. Obviously, he has perspective on blessing that no one else on the face of the planet can possibly have—so we should hang on every word he says—even when it seems counterintuitive to us.

Now, I don't want to get super technical here, but it's important we understand what *beatitude* means before we go any further.

The Beatitudes are called "the Beatitudes" in English by way of a transliteration of the Latin translation of *makarios—beatus,* which means "happy, blissful, fortunate, or flourishing."[2] Translated, the word *blessed* simply means to be made happy by God. It's not a whimsical kind of happy. *Happy* in that sense is too flimsy a word to communicate all that Jesus intended here.

John Stott said it like this: "Happiness is a subjective state, whereas Jesus is making an objective judgment."[3] Stott is distinguishing between a worldly happy and a godly happy. The happiness or blessing that Jesus is referring to in the Beatitudes is an all-weather kind of happiness. This type of blessing is bulletproof, stormproof, waterproof, tragedy-proof, and disappointment-proof. It is rooted deeply in God—not in your circumstances. Understood this way, worldly happiness fluctuates, while the blessing of happiness by God remains steadfast. Worldly happiness taps out of the fight when it gets tough, but godly happiness endures. Consequently, Jesus is establishing here that a person can be blessed-happy while still stuck in unfavorable circumstances.

Now, this runs counter to what we typically hear in prosperity gospel circles; there, a blessing always means that circumstances align. So you are blessed only when life goes smoothly.

- It's a promotion at work, not a demotion.
- It's a pay raise, not a pay cut.
- It's a bigger house, not a smaller house.

- It's a favorable doctor's report, not a scary one.

The danger in this kind of thinking comes when favorable circumstances become the *only* standard for blessing. It leads to both a deep-seated frustration and a misguided understanding of how God really works in the world. Remember, God actually uses suffering and pain and trials and struggles in order to mature our faith—which results in the blessing of maturity, perseverance, and wholeness in Christ. James elaborates on this in depth in James 1:2–4.

If you're not convinced, think about the life of Paul and the apostles; their lives were replete with suffering and trials. And they remained faithful followers of God. Bottom line, the blessed condition of a Christ-follower means that, although we are still in the world, we aren't dependent on the world to satisfy us. Our satisfaction (happiness) comes from God. And when a person's happiness and satisfaction come from God, that person is blessed, made happy by God—not by the American Dream, the right circumstances, the next sunny day, or the next big paycheck.

Specifically, Jesus declares in the first beatitude, "Blessed are the poor in spirit." To be clear, Jesus isn't glorifying material destitution. He's not saying it's awesome to be *without* in this world—and that we just need to wait to get to heaven for things to get better. To suggest this is both callous and unhelpful to anyone struggling in the here and now. Moreover, if it were true that Matthew 5:3 is referring only to material poverty, then it could be construed as un-Christian to seek to alleviate the burdens of the destitute and starving. Obviously, we know that is not right or biblical. And so, this verse does not sanction or glorify material poverty. Instead, Jesus is simply using a much-recognized financial reality to uncover a not-so-easily-recognized spiritual reality—that is, spiritual poverty.

Eugene Peterson paraphrases it this way in The Message: "You're blessed when you're at the end of your rope. With less of you there is more of God and his rule" (Matthew 5:3).

Now, I know this sounds odd; we're so used to hearing that blessing is getting to the "top of the ladder," not "the end of your rope." This feels silly, even disheartening. Yet Jesus is literally saying you are blessed when you realize that you have nothing within you that is commendable to God because yours, then, is the kingdom of heaven.

Jesus tells us this because he wants everyone to know that the kingdom of heaven will *not* be inherited by the self-righteous or the arrogant, those who think they do not need God or those who think they *are* God. The world is filled with people who are materially rich but spiritually poor. So, Jesus flips the script by saying the "hopeless cases" are actually those who *refuse* to declare their spiritual bankruptcy and subsequent need for the mercy of God. In actuality, the hopeless cases are the people who insist they've got it all together and don't need God.

So, it's not by accident that Jesus begins by blessing the spiritually inadequate (the poor in spirit) or those who embrace true poverty of spirit. You see, God continually used the poor in spirit in transformational ways; think Paul, David, Gideon, and Jesus, just to name a few. God used their surrender to weakness in amazingly strong and powerful ways.

Tragically, then, to summarily dismiss the first beatitude would be to fall prey to the Laodicean heresy of assuming we are rich and prosperous and in need of nothing—when in reality we are "pitiful, poor, blind, and naked" (Revelation 3:17, NIV).

Considering all of this, I hope this is starting to come together for you—because Christ's emphasis on being poor in spirit is designed to wean you from relying on *yourself*. It's designed to empty you (of yourself) and therefore, to highlight your need for God. The Bible is clear: rely on yourself and miss the kingdom. Rely on God and gain the kingdom. Moreover, please understand that embracing poverty of spirit is not only necessary in becoming a Christian—it's essential in growing as a Christian, too!

One way we know we are growing in Christian maturity is when our awareness of our need for God is heightened. R. Kent Hughes says it well.

Just as no one can come to Christ without poverty of spirit, no one can continue to grow apart from an ongoing poverty of spirit.

Poverty of spirit is foundational because a continual sense of spiritual need is the basis for ongoing spiritual blessing.

A perpetual awareness of our spiritual insufficiency opens us to continually receiving spiritual riches. Poverty of spirit is something we never outgrow.

In fact, the more spiritually mature we become, the more profound will be our sense of poverty.[4]

For the record, I think this beatitude is unmistakably fleshed out in Jesus' parable of the Pharisee and the tax collector in Luke 18:9–14. Here's the basic storyline: In this parable, the Pharisee trusted in himself and his own righteousness. His prayer is essentially a highlight reel of his perceived goodness. "The Pharisee, standing by himself, prayed thus: 'God, I thank you that I am not like other men, extortioners, unjust, adulterers, or even like this tax collector. I fast twice a week; I give tithes of all that I get'" (Luke 18:11–12).

By the way, can you imagine hearing someone actually pray, "I'm not like other men; extortioners, unjust, adulterers, or even like this tax collector"? It's borderline nauseating and repulsive—right?! Conversely, notice that the tax collector didn't trust in himself or compare himself to anyone else, but rather threw himself on the mercy of God. "But the tax collector, standing far off, would not even lift up his eyes to heaven, but beat his breast, saying, 'God, be merciful to me, a sinner!'" (Luke 18:13). The text concludes by saying that the Pharisee went home just as he came—self-righteous! Meanwhile, the tax collector went home justified (right with God).

Here's the reality—I think the default mode of every single human being is to try to prop ourselves up before God by comparing ourselves to others and displaying our goodness rather than laying ourselves low before God, acknowledging our neediness. In my estimation, we do this because we don't like to acknowledge our weaknesses or neediness, so we assume God must want to see our strength, our goodness, our effort.

However, God wants to see our brokenness, our honesty, our humility—and our reliance on Christ's sacrifice on the cross. And so, regardless of our spiritual maturity or biblical knowledge, embracing poverty of spirit is essential for ongoing spiritual blessing. The Bible is clear. God opposes the proud and gives grace to the humble. Pride pushes God away, while humility becomes a lightning rod for more of God's grace.

On a personal level, there have been numerous occasions where God has brought me face-to-face with my spiritual poverty and my need for him, especially as a parent. One such example happened on a picture-perfect Minnesota Sunday afternoon in July of 2017. Our family had just gotten home from a great day of worship at Grace Church when my eldest, unmarried, soon-to-be-sophomore-in-college daughter said she needed to talk. I'll never forget; as we sat down at our kitchen table, she started weeping uncontrollably and blurted out, "I am *pregnant*."

I could not believe what I was hearing. My wife Cheri and I were shocked . . . speechless . . . gutted . . . crushed . . . numb . . . and overwhelmed with pain, unlike ever before in our married lives. It was like a knife to the heart! As I sat there, stunned and in tears at our kitchen table, a million questions and thoughts raced through my mind.

- "Why?"
- "Did we fail you as parents?"
- "How could you do this?"
- "Now what?"
- "This can't be happening!"
- "What will everyone say?"
- "What about all the young girls you've been mentoring?"
- "What about your future?"
- "What about *my* future?"

I'm not sure that I've ever felt so helpless—weak and vulnerable and just plain sad. This news shook us to our core and brought us to our knees! I could barely sleep and eat. So here I was, Senior Pastor of a great church family who was really just a broken dad, absolutely brokenhearted for his daughter. Literally, this one event has reminded me of my neediness, helplessness, and poverty before the Lord. I know I am bankrupt without him. This is where I was reminded that having all the cash in the world would not have helped me through this struggle.

During those next few weeks, I found a way forward by identifying, in a small way, as Joseph with Mary. Remember, after Joseph found out Mary was pregnant, he had two goals: honor God and don't humiliate Mary. That strategy also became my position! My prayer became, "God, I want to honor You, and I don't want to publicly humiliate my daughter."

Quite honestly, it was during that season of pain that I learned more fully how God works. In particular, here's what I learned: God wants to meet our needs (according to his glorious riches), *and* at the same time, God wants us to be needy for him. It's paradoxical. God meets our needs, so we no longer have the need, yet he wants us to always recognize our need of him—which keeps us needy. I'm still figuring and fleshing this one out, by the way.

Ultimately, I'd say that the beauty and blessing of this beatitude is that God blesses us by allowing us to experience a desperate need for him, and as we embrace our neediness, God opens the door for his riches—the kingdom of heaven! How amazing is that! Knowing that you have eternal life trumps having a great retirement account any day.

Now, my guess is that you have experienced—or are currently experiencing—moments of deep brokenness in your life, too. Maybe it's a son battling a drug addiction or a daughter struggling with her gender, or a doctor's report that has left you reeling. If so, acknowledge your spiritual poverty before him. Ask him to meet your needs while keeping you needy for his person and his presence. And know this: embracing this kind of spiritual poverty will make you rich in ways you don't even know—and you'll be blessed beyond this world with the kingdom of heaven!

So, take a few moments right now to assess your level of "neediness for God". . . whatever your struggle, tell God, "I need you in my parenting—God, I need you in my marriage—God, I need you at work—God, please meet my needs and keep me needy for you!"

If you're saying to yourself, "I don't need God". . . then you *really need God!* Ask God to give you the humility to see yourself and your circumstances as they really are. Don't be like the self-righteous Pharisee, because the goal isn't self-righteousness; the goal is to be justified—made right with God.

God, please help me to lay down my pride and lean into my brokenness. Help me to see how rich I am when I acknowledge my desperate need for you. Amen!

CHAPTER 2

BLESSED ARE THOSE WHO MOURN

Blessed are those who mourn,
for they shall be comforted.
MATTHEW 5:4

On September 11, 2014, my mother, Patsy Dobbs, died of liver cancer. She was 70 years old. We had a really special relationship for one big reason. You see, really early on in my parents' marriage, my mother—and father—endured through and agonized over four miscarriages. Finally, they had a daughter, but she only lived 24 hours before passing away. Her name was Renee Lynn Dobbs. Obviously, they were both heartbroken—grieved and devastated by their crushing losses. A few years later, all of this prompted my mom and dad to ride out a lengthy adoption process—finally adopting me.

And—I think—because my mom had faced so much grief, hurt, and loss, she had a lot of pent up mothering to do!

And mothering she did!

She literally treated me like a gift from the Lord. She'd do anything for me, from making me food at any time during the day or night to rebounding free throws for hours. She led me to Christ and urged me to trust my life to him. When I was growing up, she even *ironed* my underwear. I remember every time I would visit her, even as a 40-year-old man, she would slip me a 20-dollar bill. My mom was my biggest cheerleader. And to this day, my siblings, Toni and Tracy, will say that I was the "golden child."

So, when she died, it nearly crushed me. The grief was overwhelming. I had an ache in my soul. I could barely speak at her funeral as I delivered the funeral message. I didn't question the Lord—I just hurt. And I'm sure many of you can relate to those emotions, having lost loved ones, too. The grief is suffocating.

During that season of grieving, I was actually preaching a series through the gospel of Matthew, specifically Matthew 5:4 where it says, "Blessed are those who mourn, for they shall be comforted."

As I began to unpack this verse for my own situation, I read the words of one Bible commentator, who pointed out something I hadn't realized—he said Jesus was not referring to the sorrow of bereavement—but rather to the sorrow of repentance. The idea behind this beatitude is that we'd grieve over our own sins in the same way we grieve over the death of a loved one.

As I dug into this, I found that, of the nine words for *sorrow* in the Bible, this word *mourn*, or *pentheo* in the Greek, is the strongest of all. It means to grieve or lament. It denotes an aching and grieving for the dead or for a severe and painful loss. In verse 4, Jesus is saying that God actually blesses us by allowing us to experience deep sorrow *over the sins* that have made us so needy for God in the first place. Literally, Jesus is saying blessing comes as we mourn over our sins in the way we'd mourn over the loss of a loved one!

In fact, one bona fide mark of a follower of Jesus Christ is that she does not excuse, rationalize, trivialize, belittle, or ignore sin. Rather, she grieves over it, confesses it, and repents of it. And make no mistake, it is a gift of grace when we can have the right perspective on sin, which in turn prompts us to react and respond to our sin appropriately.

So let me ask you about it. How seriously do you take your sin? Do you hate it? Do you grieve it? Or do you love it, ignore it, traffic in it—even trivialize it?

My guess is that we all know people who've mourned over being *caught in sin.* Maybe that's you—are you mourning and grieving, not because you've sinned, but because you've been busted by your parents, your teachers, your coach, the police, or someone else in a position of authority? We probably all know people who've mourned over the consequences of sin. Some mourn over the loss of privileges, freedoms, paychecks, relationships, and jobs. But that doesn't necessarily mean they've mourned over their sin.

To be clear, Jesus is saying we miss the point when we mourn more over what we've lost than over what we've done. Please reread that sentence again—it's hugely important to grasp what it means. Mourning over anything other than our sin is missing the heart of this beatitude—completely. It is still a failure to take sin seriously.

Let me test your Bible knowledge a little here. Do you remember what happened to King Saul in the Old Testament? After the king disobeyed God's command, the prophet Samuel confronted him over his sinful rebellion, to which Saul replied, "I have sinned. I violated the LORD's command and your instructions. I was afraid of the men and so I gave in to them. Now I beg you, forgive my sin and come back with me, so that I may worship the LORD" (1 Samuel 15:24–25, NIV). At first glance, Saul's response sounds legitimate, but as you dig a little deeper, you'll actually see that Saul's confession of mouth was faster than his contrition of heart. He didn't genuinely grieve over his sin. He actually made an excuse for his sin: "I was afraid of the men and so I gave in to them" (verse 24). You see, Saul basically wanted to get the public scandal out of the way as soon as possible so that he could appear holy before the people once again . . . which is not the same as mourning over sin. And that's true of a lot of people; they'd rather get it over with than genuinely grieve it. We'd all rather get back to the party instead of getting right with God.

By way of contrast, another from the Old Testament, David, expressed grief to God over his sin against Uriah—murder—and

Bathsheba—adultery. "For I know my transgressions, and my sin is always before me. Against you, you only, have I sinned and done what is evil in your sight; so you are right in your verdict and justified when you judge" (Psalm 51:3–4, NIV). Notice that David's not dropping a million excuses on anyone. Nor is there in David an attitude of "Let's hurry up and get this over with" response. He is completely honest with himself and with God regarding his sin.

We learn a valuable lesson here. A broken heart over sin is a prerequisite for genuine confession of sin. David understood that completely. David understood that sin is ultimately an offense against a holy God. With that in mind, our mourning over sin must emerge out of that reality; it is God who is offended by our sin.

Additionally, from my vantage point, it seems people rarely get specific when addressing their thoughts, their attitudes, their language, their lust, their disobedience, their greed, their pride—their sin. In that regard, Puritan Thomas Watson stated, "A wicked man will say he is a sinner, but a child of God says, I have done this evil."[5] Here we see how specificity in describing sin speaks to our understanding of the seriousness of sin. Give this some thought in your own walk with Christ. Are you generic or specific in the confession of your sin? Do you lump them all together and dump them before God . . . or do you confess them individually as someone really broken by each sin and its offense to God? Take a moment right now and specifically list those sins you've committed this week—this morning! Come clean. Christ will forgive you and comfort you.

As I thought about this beatitude, another passage from the Old Testament kept coming to my mind. My guess is that it's not a passage people read for fun or inspiration, but it has something important to say to us about the second beatitude. Please don't cringe or put this book down; but in the first few chapters of Leviticus, you see various types of offerings defined in great detail. The first was the burnt offering; there, the animal served as the symbolic substitute for the sinner who seeks to approach the holy God of Israel.

I know this isn't an easy read, but take five minutes to study this passage—I promise it'll be worth your time.

If the offering is a burnt offering from the herd, you are to offer a male without defect. You must present it at the entrance to the tent of meeting so that it will be acceptable to the LORD. You are to lay your hand on the head of the burnt offering, and it will be accepted on your behalf to make atonement for you. You are to slaughter the young bull before the LORD, and then Aaron's sons the priests shall bring the blood and splash it against the sides of the altar at the entrance to the tent of meeting. You are to skin the burnt offering and cut it into pieces. The sons of Aaron the priest are to put fire on the altar and arrange wood on the fire. Then Aaron's sons the priests shall arrange the pieces, including the head and the fat, on the wood that is burning on the altar. You are to wash the internal organs and the legs with water, and the priest is to burn all of it on the altar. It is a burnt offering, a food offering, an aroma pleasing to the LORD.

—Leviticus 1:3–9, NIV

Let me ask you this question: How do you think you would feel about your sin while you watched this act being played out right before your eyes? You'd certainly get an up-close-and-personal sense of the dreadful seriousness of your sins, wouldn't you? The blood. The pain. The smells. The sounds. The death.

Please don't miss that, in this act, it was the sinner himself who had to kill the sacrifice and then watch as the sons of Aaron the priest drained the blood and sprinkled it all over the altar. From there, he also had to watch as the animal was divided in such a meticulous manner, with fat and entrails taken out and spread upon the wood of the altar. What a sobering pageant of blood and death it would be to watch, especially knowing that it was being done because of *your* sins! How vividly the cost of your sin would be displayed before you, in all its bloody, gory detail!

As I read this description in Leviticus, I thought, "How could anyone making such an offering for sin do so without going through a deep sense of personal, inward grief and mourning for their sins?" And that's exactly the point! Sin is a big deal because it requires the shedding of blood to secure forgiveness.

Today we live in the age of grace where that entire sacrificial system has given way to the greatest sacrifice of all time: Christ dying on the cross for our sins! The point is this—if I am moved by the blood of the animals, how much more should I be moved by the blood of the Savior Jesus Christ? How could I not experience a great mourning, sorrow, and remorse over my sins that cost Jesus his life? If I'm truly a follower of Christ, how could I be indifferent, insensitive, or hard-hearted to the incalculable price Christ paid for my sins—his very life?!

The Beatitudes show us that once we realize the poverty of our own souls, we should also feel grief and remorse for our sins. Now, let's just go ahead and say it: mourning is unpleasant. Everyone wants to party—no one wants to mourn.

Rarely do we think of mourners as blessed. We typically see them as people to be pitied or helped. We see them as in need of a casserole . . . but here we are encouraged to see them as people *to be envied.* And here's why: As you mourn over your sins, Christ himself comes alongside you to bless and forgive and strengthen you. *He, himself, gives comfort.* Think of it this way: When you take your sin seriously, Christ doesn't leave you hanging—he comforts you and blesses you by forgiving you! Jesus can comfort us like *no one else* can because Christ deals completely with the sin over which we mourn. Jesus Christ cleanses us from the penalty, the presence, the power of sin.

This is why King David used the word *blessed* when he talked about being forgiven. "Blessed is the one whose transgressions are forgiven, whose sins are covered. Blessed is the one whose sin the LORD does not count against them and in whose spirit is no deceit" (Psalm 32:1–2, NIV). The truth of the matter is that when we don't mourn and confess sin, it weakens us physically. Consider these words from Psalm 32: "When I kept silent [didn't confess], my bones wasted away through my groaning all day long. For day and night your hand was heavy on me; my strength was sapped as in the heat of summer" (Psalm 32:3–4, NIV).

The bottom line is this: Christians take their sins seriously because God takes them seriously! And as we take them seriously, we, like David, will be personally blessed and comforted by Christ with the forgiveness of God. Hopefully, you are starting to see what true happiness and blessing looks like in the Beatitudes. It's a most counterintuitive way to think and live. Typically, people erroneously think true happiness means luxury, leisure, long vacations, and the easy life . . . not poverty of spirit and mourning over our sins. But God has a deep blessing in store for those who take their sins seriously—and that blessing is his forgiveness of our sins.

In all honesty, I'm not sure I've ever grieved over my sins the way Jesus refers to in this beatitude. I confess my sins—yes. But this beatitude has forced me—and I hope it'll force you—to take your sins far more seriously, knowing *our* sins cost Christ *his* life. Moreover, I hope you'll see the beauty in this beatitude: God forgives our sins. There is no sin too great that God can't or won't forgive.

With all this in mind, let's stop numbing ourselves with entertainment. Let's stop making excuses and just be real. Let's stop being bound by shame and guilt, and instead walk in the freedom that is ours in Christ Jesus. Take a few moments right now to bring your specific sins before Christ. Think about why he died; the Bible says Christ died for our sins, and *because of* our sins. Our sins sent Christ to the cross. We are guilty, but he is willing to take away our sins and our guilt. Let's treat Christ seriously by taking our sins seriously!

God, please help me take my sins more seriously. Allow me the grace of seeing how my sin impacted your Son, my Savior. Help me to mourn, confess, and repent of my sin in a way that reflects my understanding of Christ's sacrifice on the cross! Amen.

CHAPTER 3

BLESSED ARE THE MEEK

Blessed are the meek, for they will inherit the earth.
MATTHEW 5:5, NIV

Everyone loves power; from my house to your house to the White House—power intoxicates. People will do nearly anything to get power—and keep it.

If you aren't convinced people are into power, just spend five minutes scanning the American landscape for examples. There's the PowerBar®, the power tie, the power trip, the power walk, power tools, the power wash, Powerade®, Powerball®, the Power Juicer™, PowerPoint® (you don't just make a point; you make a PowerPoint), and one of my personal favorites—the power nap!

Make no mistake about it—people love power and what it represents: identity, celebrity, and status. People want to be strong and dominant because it gives them the illusion of being in control.

Ultimately, I think it's why so many people struggle with this beatitude: "Blessed are the meek, for they will inherit the earth." Most people tend to believe that meekness is weakness, and who wants to be weak? Or they think meekness may work in the church, but it won't fly in the real world. They believe the only thing the meek get is smacked around or left behind.

Well, if that's you, you'll be pleasantly surprised, because meek doesn't mean anything close to the descriptions above.

Specifically, being meek does not imply timidity, frailty, a lack of conviction, or seeking peace at any cost. It does not mean soft or spineless. It doesn't mean that you become the proverbial doormat for people to walk over.

Moreover, if you think you're the only one who takes umbrage with the word *meek*, you are wrong. Remember, in Matthew's gospel, Jesus' target audience was the Jewish community, and their expectation was a Braveheart, William Wallace-esque, Navy-SEAL-like messiah who would annihilate their hated Roman oppressors! In their minds, great causes were fought by the strong—not the meek. That's why the Beatitudes are hard to embrace; they thought you could not win victories while mourning, and you certainly could never conquer Rome without toughness and power. So the phrase *blessed are the meek* would no doubt have been met with a rousing "Are you kidding me?" response by Jesus' original audience.

One author writes,

In whatever way various groups of people expected the Messiah to come, they did not anticipate His coming humbly and meekly. . . . The idea of a meek Messiah leading meek people was far from any of their concepts of the messianic kingdom. The Jews understood military power and miracle power. . . . But they did not understand the power of meekness. . . . In spite of all the miracles of His ministry, the people never really believed in Him as the Messiah, because He failed to act in military or miracle power against Rome. . . . That was not the kind of Messiah they wanted.[6]

Truth be told, most of us still don't understand the power of meekness. And most of us still struggle with the New Testament Jesus—and his ministry in the world.

Besides, if the word *meek* doesn't mean weak, soft, or spineless, then what exactly does it mean? We certainly can't understand this beatitude without rightly interpreting this word. The Greek for *meek* is a word that means "power under control," "bridled strength," or "power harnessed for a purpose." Think in terms of a wild horse that needs to be broken to be made useful to its owner. A meek horse, then, is not a weak horse—but rather a thriving beast brought under its master's control.

Additionally, this beatitude mirrors the promise in Psalm 37:11 (a messianic psalm) where it says, "But the meek will inherit the land and enjoy peace and prosperity" (NIV). In this verse, the equivalent Hebrew word for *meek* is used to describe someone who is submissive to the will of God. The meek person then, is not a weak person, but rather one who demonstrates power under control and submission to God.

In order to add some color to the definition of *meekness*, let's examine two biblical examples who personified biblical meekness: Joseph and Jesus. Joseph's story is found in Genesis, Chapters 37–50. He was the favored son of his father, Jacob. The Bible reveals that Jacob loved Joseph more than his brothers for two reasons: first, he had been born to him in his old age, and second, Joseph's mother was Jacob's favored wife, Rachel. Now here's the thing: being the favorite is great—if you're the favorite. But if you're one of the forgotten siblings, favoritism hurts and alienates and breeds resentment. Not surprisingly, over time, Joseph's brothers grew to despise him. The tipping point was a combination of two issues: the coat of many colors he received as a gift from Jacob, and his continually telling his brothers, "Hey, guys, I have to tell you, I keep having these dreams, and in these dreams, you all bow down before me."

Joseph's brothers had had enough. Literally! As the story goes, while away from home and the protective covering of Jacob, they made the decision to kill their brother. However, at the last moment they were persuaded by Reuben, the eldest, to sell him off into slavery instead. After this treacherous act of human trafficking, they returned home and delivered a concocted—well-rehearsed—story to Jacob about how Joseph was destroyed by a wild animal . . . using, ironically, the bloody, dirty coat of many colors as Exhibit A. In hearing this devasting news, Jacob was inconsolable—he was undone. The brothers feigned a season of grief but were glad he was gone.

However, Joseph was not dead, and God was not done using him. Through a series of (providentially painful) events—false accusations, unjust imprisonment, and being forgotten to name a few—God eventually positioned Joseph as second in command in Egypt. In fact, God used Joseph's ability to interpret dreams to set him apart as Pharaoh's go-to guy. Not only that, but God used Joseph's administrative skills to preserve the region—including his brothers—from a terrible seven-year famine.

Years later, as Joseph stood face-to-face with his brothers, it was a God-inspired meekness that allowed him to look beyond the murderous intentions and brutally cruel actions of his brothers. Instead he looked to the sovereignty of God. And so when his brothers came to Egypt in search of food, Joseph immediately recognized them—but they didn't recognize him. Why would they? They had left him for dead. When the moment of truth arrived with the unveiling of his true identity, Joseph didn't hammer his brothers for their atrocities against him. Amazingly, he processed all of his brothers' dealings with him without toxic bitterness and unhinged revenge in his heart.

Rather, we read his meek response. "But Joseph said to them, 'Don't be afraid. Am I in the place of God? You intended to harm me, but God intended it for good to accomplish what is now being done, the saving of many lives'" (Genesis 50:19–20, NIV). His brothers justifiably feared for their lives, but in meekness, Joseph restrained from taking revenge. He modeled "power under control." In lieu of seeking revenge, he only spoke of the sovereignty of God and God's greater purposes. I like to think that he had self-control because he believed God was in control. I love that thought, don't you? You and I can have self-control because God is in control. As we embrace the sovereignty of God *over* our lives, it can lead to a self-controlled meekness *in* our lives.

While we might be rightly impressed with Joseph's meekness, Jesus is the perfect example of bridled strength for the good of others. Jesus held all the power in the universe in his hands but willingly and lovingly held back that power to give his life on the cross as an atoning sacrifice for sin. His friend Peter had much to say about Jesus as Jesus approached the final hours of his life. "'He committed no sin, and no deceit was found in his mouth.' When they hurled their insults at him, he did not retaliate; when he suffered, he made no threats. Instead, he entrusted himself *to him who judges justly*" (1 Peter 2:22–23, NIV, emphasis added). Notice the text says Jesus did not retaliate. He made no threats, but rather he surrendered to the brutality of the cross because he knew his Father would judge justly. Above all else, Jesus trusted in the sovereign plan and goodness of God as he endured the agony of the cross. And so, like Joseph, we could say that Jesus, too, had self-control because he knew God was in control. We know he had the power—in a word—to destroy his accusers and enemies. But he chose restraint and submission to the will of God instead of revenge and malice and destruction.

Consequently—and don't miss this—both Joseph and Jesus modeled meekness by surrendering their struggles, their futures, their questions—even their pain—to God. Accordingly, embracing meekness creates in each of us a controlled, gentle, trusting spirit rooted in an unshakable confidence in the goodness and sovereignty of God. This is really important to know, because when you have an unshakable confidence in the goodness and sovereignty of God, it will enable you to remain meek and gentle when maligned, attacked, or provoked. Even if your world is spinning out of control, you know God is in control, so you can trust him and rest in him. You can count on him.

My guess is that many of you reading this right now need to hear this again: God is in control, so you can stop pacing. God doesn't sleep, so you can finally get some sleep. God is in charge! If family, friends, co-workers, or enemies betray, attack, or slander your name, you don't have to stress out, get the last word, complain, yell, or use force or intimidation or exploitation to get your way—because God is in control of every facet of your life! Instead, you can exercise meekness and restraint because God has you in his plan and care. God knows what is going on—in you and around you.

For me, the most surprising truth from the lives of Joseph and Jesus is that a Spirit-driven meekness allows for boldness in the face of evil. Did you notice that neither Joseph nor Jesus wavered or cowered in the face of evil? Instead, they framed up their trials—even the evil intent of their enemies—in light of God's goodness and sovereignty. They knew that humanity is not in control and evil does not have the last word.

For Joseph, the struggles, the betrayals, and the imprisonment gave way to Pharaoh's palace and family reconciliation—and being used by God to save countless lives from starvation. For Jesus, the agony of the cross gave way to the resurrection and the salvation of many—plus the ultimate recognition from God (and one day the whole world!) that Jesus is King of Kings and Lord of Lords. Bottom line, whatever you're going through today—cancer, divorce, betrayal, bankruptcy, foreclosure, job loss—know this: God knows, God cares, and God is greater than your greatest struggle. God is good, and he is in control.

Most of us, if we are not careful, tend to live life feeling as if we are owed something or that we are entitled to the best of everything. However, Martyn Lloyd-Jones said, "The one who is truly meek is the one who is amazed that God and people think of them as well as they do, and treat them as well as they do!"[7] As such, one who embraces meekness realizes it becomes a stabilizing force that keeps us from thinking too highly of ourselves and from always expecting a break. Rather, meekness says something altogether different. "If there's a job that no one wants to do, I'll do it. If there's a kid who no one wants to eat lunch with, I'll eat with that kid. If there's a hardship I have to endure, I'll go through it for God's glory. If there's a sacrifice someone needs to make, I'll make it."

Keep in mind that the meek person doesn't do this out of guilt, under compulsion, or in a spirit of martyrdom. He does it because he is absolutely convinced that God is good and in complete control of all things. Obviously, this kind of meekness doesn't come naturally to us. Yet, Joseph and Jesus both experienced that God always gives what's best to those who entrust their lives to his sovereign control—hence the phrase: "he entrusted himself to him who judges justly." Jesus knew God would bring ultimate justice. And Joseph found this to be true in his life, as well.

To be clear, when Jesus says, "Blessed are the meek, for they will inherit the earth," please know that he is not referring to things like wealth, fame, or fast cars—things that people deem as essential. Ultimately, the Bible tells us that "the earth is the LORD's, and everything in it" (Psalm 24:1, NIV). "The earth" includes all the good things that God has made and all the good gifts he offers to his children, like beauty, meaning, love, joy, purpose, significance, and salvation. "The earth" represents the goodness and fullness of God, both in this life and the life to come.

As well, notice when Jesus says, "They will inherit the earth." *Inherit* is an interesting word choice here, don't you think? What do you have to do to inherit something? Nothing. In fact, the moment you start pursuing your inheritance, something's wrong. When you start pushing someone or ingratiating yourself to someone in the hope that they'll put you in their will, then you've probably disqualified yourself from the inheritance and instead created a really awkward moment! Literally, the only way to inherit something is to be rightly related to the person who has something to give away. And the only way to inherit the earth is to be rightly related to the One who owns the earth: God himself! But remember, you can't become rightly related to God until you personally know the Son of God, Jesus Christ.

According to Matthew 5:5, the best is yet to come for the meek because someday the meek will assume their inheritance. Think about that: *The best is yet to come!* If it's tough for you, it'll get better. If it's good for you, it'll get even better.

So, blessed are the meek, for they will inherit the earth *after the proud have killed themselves trying to possess it.*

R. Kent Hughes stated, "We should note that poverty of spirit and mourning are negative. However, when true poverty of spirit and spiritual mourning are present, they make way for the positive virtue of meekness. In a sense, meekness is superior to the two preceding states because it grows out of them. The process is all so natural, so beautiful, and yet also quite supernatural!"[8]

Let's connect the dots for a moment. When genuine poverty of spirit (beatitude 1) is accompanied by mourning over sin (beatitude 2), these two realities create in us a gentleness and a meekness (beatitude 3), both in the way we respond to the Lord Jesus and in the way we treat others after we've been mistreated. So know this: embracing the Beatitudes will change you forever.

Be encouraged to know this—God's new creation will not be possessed by powerful kings, ruthless dictators, manipulative politicians, high-powered athletes, or the Hollywood elite.

It will be possessed by the meek, not the strong or dominant.

And so, when the heat is on, let's choose restraint over revenge. Let's be energized by his sovereignty. Let's confidently rest in the unshakable, immovable character and power of the Lord Jesus Christ. And let's not shun meekness—let's embrace meekness: a bridled strength, a self-control that restrains itself because of an unshakable confidence in the goodness and sovereignty of God.

Let's stop seeking to get and maintain power. Instead, rely on the One who has all the power, Jesus Christ.

God, help me not to believe the lie that my top goal in life is to gain and keep power. Please give me the willingness to surrender my heart to meekness. Thank you for being in control of my life from beginning to end. Amen.

CHAPTER 4

BLESSED ARE THOSE WHO HUNGER AND THIRST FOR RIGHTEOUSNESS

Blessed are those who hunger and thirst for
righteousness, for they will be filled.
MATTHEW 5:6, NIV

If you haven't started to wrestle with some of the bigger questions of life, I hope you will soon. You know what I mean; these are important things to consider. Why am I here on earth? What is my purpose in life? Am I doing anything to make a difference in the world? What will my legacy be when I'm gone?

Obviously, those are all hugely important questions to think through and figure out for yourself. And yet from a biblical perspective, there's not a bigger or more relevant question for all of humanity than this one: How do I know whether or not I really know Jesus Christ?

This question may lead to others. Can I really know? Is it that important to know? To which I would say, "Yes!" and, "Yes!"

Please understand me—if you are a follower of Jesus Christ, uncertainty in your mind and your heart regarding your relationship with Christ will lead to inconsistency and ineffectiveness in your walk with him. Think of it like this: if I am struggling to *trust* that Christ is in me and for me, chances are I won't *live* like Christ is in me and for me. Assurance of salvation is indispensable to a blessed Christian experience. Every Christ-follower must settle this issue once and for all time.

Moreover—and this is *huge*—prolonged uncertainty and uneasiness regarding your status with Christ may indicate that you don't really *know* Christ. The Holy Spirit may be gently letting you know that you are still in need of a true relationship with Jesus. If that is the case, don't fight it—submit to it. Surrender your life to Jesus Christ; by faith, confess your sins and trust in who Christ is and all that Christ has done—right now!

Fortunately for us, the next beatitude perfectly sets forth the answer to the question, "How can I know that I know Jesus Christ?" Martyn Lloyd-Jones said it like this: "I do not know of a better test that anyone can apply to himself or herself in this whole matter of the Christian profession than a verse like this."[9]

So let's look together at the verse he's referencing: "Blessed are those who hunger and thirst for righteousness, for they will be filled" (Matthew 5:6, NIV).

One answer to the question, "How can I know that I really know Jesus Christ?" then, is this: your desires will change. Charles Spurgeon used to say, "True godliness lies very much in our desires."[10] Said another way, what you hunger and thirst for says a lot about who you are and where you stand with Jesus Christ. It shouldn't come as a surprise to anyone that our cravings (what we want) lead to our choices (what we do), which in turn sets the trajectory of our lives (where we are going).

My guess is that not everyone reading this book has experienced true hunger or thirst. I don't know that I ever have, either. For most of us, hunger means waiting an extra ten minutes before we're seated at the restaurant. Or it's the typical teenager, who—fifteen minutes after a Thanksgiving feast—is rummaging through the kitchen looking for food while saying, "I'm starving." We know it's a figure of speech, not a cold, hard reality, right? Truthfully, we Americans are the best-fed people on the planet. We're overfed. We are so used to not being hungry that our preoccupation is instead with losing weight instead of getting something to eat or drink. In fact, today, many people spend more money on trying to lose weight than on buying food. If we're thirsty, all we do is turn on the faucet for cold, refreshing water. If we're hungry, we just open the refrigerator and go for it.

Not so with Jesus' original listening audience; they were never far from the stark reality of starvation or dehydration. Accordingly, then, I think it's easy for us to miss the punch and urgency of these words. Jesus is *not* painting a comfortable picture, either physically or spiritually. *Starvation* and *desperation* are never pretty terms. And so we need to let them sink in.

In addition, if we want to understand the fourth beatitude, we also need to know what Jesus meant by the term *righteousness*. Interpretively speaking, the rule of thumb is this: if you come across a section of the Bible you don't understand, then look to other passages of Scripture for elucidation because Scripture interprets Scripture.

With that in mind, let's look at four other uses of the word *righteousness* in Jesus' Sermon on the Mount. In Matthew 5:10, NIV, Jesus said, "Blessed are those who are persecuted because of righteousness." As you combine the fourth and eighth beatitudes, it reads like this: We are to hunger and thirst after a kind of righteous life that will cause some people to persecute us for our faith in Christ. Thus, righteousness is a lifestyle that not only sets us apart as true Christians, but also invites subsequent opposition from the world.

The second use of the word *righteousness* comes from Matthew 5:20, NIV. "For I tell you that unless your righteousness surpasses that of the Pharisees and the teachers of the law, you will certainly not enter the kingdom of heaven." In the first century, the Pharisees developed an elaborate religious system built around superficial, meticulous, moralistic, external standards. Because of this, Jesus often challenged them to stop elevating their rules above God's Word. *Righteousness* in this context isn't defined by what we do or don't do; it comes from what Christ has done on the cross.

Next, Matthew 6:1 gives us the third use of the word *righteousness*. "Beware of practicing your righteousness before other people in order to be seen by them, for then you will have no reward from your Father who is in heaven." Many Pharisees loved the limelight. They prayed in order to be seen praying. They loved to dress up in their religious garb and throw their offerings into the metal containers so that people could hear their "generosity" and be impressed with their religiosity. Some would sacrifice nearly anything to win the approval and applause of others. Their religion was built on the praise of men. It was form over substance with them. By contrast, Jesus says a true disciple seeks a righteousness that doesn't need to be seen by others, but only by God.

Lastly, Matthew 6:33, NIV, says this about righteousness: "But seek first his kingdom and his righteousness, and all these things will be given to you as well." Matthew 6 concludes a section of Scripture in which Jesus taught about the worries of life—especially worrying over the future. In this passage, Jesus says that no matter what worries you, the antidote for worry is seeking the kingdom of God and his righteousness above everything else.

My paraphrase of Matthew 6:33 is this: *Aim your life at your Father—not your future—and your Father will take care of your future.* Sadly, most of us tend to focus our energy on an unknown or unknowable future, which, in turn, creates worry in our hearts. Instead, Jesus says to focus your energy, your life on your heavenly Father and his righteousness, and all the things you are worrying about will be added to you.

To summarize, the word *righteousness* from the Sermon on the Mount means several things.

1. Being in a right relationship with God through Christ comes because of who Christ is and what he has done— not because of what we do or don't do.
2. Living a righteous Christian lifestyle will ultimately invite opposition from the world.
3. We should want our righteousness to please God, not gain the applause of man.
4. Making God's righteous agenda on earth should be our top priority.

So how, then, do you know—really know—that you are right with Jesus based on this beatitude? Remember Spurgeon's statement: "True godliness lies very much in desires."

What did he mean?

While I haven't talked to him personally (as he's been dead for over 125 years), I think he was saying that our desires reveal our allegiances and our commitments and our approach to righteousness. You may see yourself in one of the statements below.

- "I used to have **no desire** for corporate worship (and used to look for ways to get out of it), but now I crave it."
- "I used to have **no desire** for the Scriptures; now I can't do without them. I love God's Word!"
- "I used to have **no desire** for the gospel, but now I think about sharing it with others all the time."
- "I used to have **no desire** to leave the United States, but now I want to take the gospel to the nations!"
- "I used to have **no desire** to know or follow Christ, but now it's my *top* priority!"

In no uncertain terms, your desires are revealing. They reveal your passions and allegiances. They reveal what's important and valuable and meaningful to you. We cannot escape this connection between our desires and allegiances and what's important to us.

Over the years, I've learned that *one* all-consuming desire (whether good or bad) has the capacity to swallow up all the rest. For example, I grew up in the State of Indiana where basketball is *everything*. Basketball is so over-the-top *crazy* there that it is even referred to as *Hoosier Hysteria*! During my own teenage years, my passion for basketball swallowed up everything. It swallowed up my schoolwork, hygiene, friendships, and future decisions. It was an all-encompassing desire that revealed much about me. It impacted how I spent my time, how I spent my money, what I did on the weekends, and who I hung around.

Whether it's sports, fishing, recreation, family, money, or even work—whatever it is—your top desire can cannibalize all the rest. So, what is it for you? What are you obsessed with the most? What do you crave more than anything else? What do you live for? What are you willing to die for? What receives your best effort and energy? Is it Jesus—or something or someone else?

Here's the truth: only *you* know if you really desire God. I don't know what's really going on in your heart, or what you think of God! Yes, I can look at your life and make educated guesses, but I don't *know* what's in your heart. Only you really know, so be honest with yourself. Don't risk playing around with something of such magnitude.

The Bible teaches that a genuine conversion to Christianity will be marked by a radical shift in desires. So my desires will either point to my love for and allegiance to the person of Jesus Christ or they will not. Another way to know we are right with Jesus is marked by an intense desperation in our hearts for Christ to make things right in our culture. Let me ask you straight up— have you come to the place in life where you really desire for Jesus to make right every wrong, make right every injustice, and make right everything contrary to his will and Word? If so, then your desire for righteousness reveals your growth in righteousness.

Here's the million-dollar question: Can you truthfully say, "I long to know Christ's righteousness as a starving man longs for food and water"?

That's intense, isn't it?

We all know that a starving person has a single-minded, all-consuming passion for food and water. All other desires pale in comparison. Nothing else has the slightest attraction or appeal, and nothing else can even capture a person's attention. You want it so strongly you feel the pangs deep within your soul. It's a matter of life and death. Your very existence depends on that *one* cup of water or that *one* bite of bread. This is the imagery Jesus employs for the way we are to pursue Christ and his righteousness in our culture.

In my estimation, Jesus' words absolutely *gut* the "cultural Christianity" we see in America today. The Beatitudes scream to those who treat Christ and his church as optional or irrelevant; to those guilty of theological or biblical dilettantism; to those with a half-hearted commitment to the Word of God and Son of God—to wake up and get serious about Christ!

You see—and this is frightening to me—there is a kind of "knowing" ("knowing" Christ) that is not New Testament Christianity at all. And here's why: The Bible clearly teaches that spiritual hunger follows new birth. The Apostle Peter said it like this: "Like newborn babies, crave pure spiritual milk, so that by it you may grow up in your salvation" (1 Peter 2:2, NIV). Here's the point: If you are genuinely converted, you won't need to be unnaturally manipulated to desire the Word—you will come out of the spiritual womb *craving* it . . . just as a baby craves its mother's milk.

By God's grace, in February of 2018, our first grandson was born. His name is Jax, and he's awesome. Jax loves to eat—as a baby he had fat rolls on his ankles to prove it—and right out of the womb, he instinctively began searching for a food source. He had a built-in desire for food. We never had to push him to be hungry. As a matter of fact, he always let us know when he was hungry. His lungs were quite well-developed for a little guy.

In the same way—spiritually speaking—if you have no desire to consume the Word or to worship God, then you aren't in a good place with Christ. If your appetite for the things of God isn't there—check yourself. Ask God—ask others—to help you. Right now.

On the positive side, don't miss an important point. In your desperation for Jesus Christ, you also get the satisfaction that you desperately need. "Blessed are those who hunger and thirst for righteousness, *for they will be filled*" (emphasis added). Those who hunger and thirst for righteousness will be filled with righteousness. They'll be made right with God. How amazing is that, right? As I hunger and thirst for God—God fills me up to the point of satisfaction in and through him.

Considering this, can I encourage you to assess your level of desperation for Christ—or lack thereof? Doing so will tell you what you need to know—and what you need to do next.

In closing, A.W. Tozer really helped me to *get* Matthew 5:6. In quoting Browning, Tozer stated,

Hunger is a pain. It is God's merciful provision, a divinely sent stimulus to propel us in the direction of food. If food-hunger is a pain, thirst, which is water-hunger, is a hundredfold worse, and the more critical the need becomes within the living organism the more acute the pain. It is nature's last drastic effort to rouse the imperiled life to seek to renew itself. A dead body feels no hunger and the dead soul knows not the pangs of holy desire. "If you want God," said the old saint, "you have already found Him." Our desire for fuller life is proof that some life must be there already. Our very dissatisfactions should encourage us, our yet unfulfilled aspirations should give us hope. "What I aspired to be, and was not, comforts me."[11]

Friend—I hope you love knowing that God has given us tangible ways to know whether or not we actually know him. God wants us to have the assurance of salvation! God wants us to know that we know we are right with him.

To that end, I love reading amongst the last words of Scripture where this amazing invitation is given by God. "The Spirit and the bride say, 'Come!' And let the one who hears say, 'Come!' Let the one who is thirsty come; and let the one who wishes take the free gift of the water of life" (Revelation 22:17, NIV). Please know—if you've never thirsted for righteousness, if that desire is not in you and has never been in you, then *come and drink* freely, receiving God's free gift of salvation through his Son, Jesus Christ.

If you've already trusted Christ, then let this beatitude broaden your understanding of blessing to include hungering and thirsting for righteousness—hungering for people to be right with God and hungering for God to make things right on earth—because when you do, you will be filled and satisfied and blessed like never before!

God, please help me to assess my spiritual thirst and hunger for your righteousness. Please give me a voracious appetite for the gospel and for people who are without you. Please give me the assurance of my salvation and a certainty in my position before you. Please help me to pursue righteousness in my daily life. Amen.

CHAPTER 5

BLESSED ARE THE MERCIFUL

> Blessed are the merciful, for they
> will be shown mercy.
> MATTHEW 5:7, NIV

Mercy is a beautiful and noble concept; however, for a lot of people, it never leaves the concept phase! For many of us, it's just way easier to be *done* with people than it is to be merciful to them. It's way easier to check out relationally than it is to work things out relationally.

Not long ago, I stumbled across an old story about a priest who welcomed a weary traveler into his home. After learning that his guest was almost one hundred years old, the priest asked about his religious beliefs.

The man replied, "I'm an atheist."

Infuriated, the priest forced the man out, saying, "I will not harbor an atheist in my house." Without a word, the elderly man hobbled out into the darkness.

As the priest sat down to read the Scriptures that evening, he heard the voice of God say, "Son, why did you throw that man out?"

"Because he is an atheist, and I cannot endure him overnight," he answered.

To which God replied, "I have endured him for almost a hundred years. You can at least extend mercy to him for one night."

At that, the priest rushed out and treated him with compassion and mercy.

The moral of the story is that mercy is great in theory . . . but tough to put into practice.

You may have noticed it seems there is something in all of us that would rather pay someone back than give someone a second chance—especially if that person has hurt or offended us or someone we love.

On a personal note, it took me several years to work through not just being "done" with people who hurt me. Having been adopted, I struggled with deep rejection issues and learned how to end relationships instead of enduring in them. So this beatitude has been a lifesaver for me.

In order to help us keep our bearings, please notice that the first four beatitudes focus primarily on the believer's relationship with God, while the next four, beginning with verse 7, focus on the believer's relationships with other people. This mirrors the Great Commandment, where we are to love God and love people. Jesus told us this in Matthew 22:37–40. "And he said to him, 'You shall love the Lord your God with all your heart and with all your soul and with all your mind. This is the great and first commandment. And a second is like it: You shall love your neighbor as yourself. On these two commandments depend all the Law and the Prophets.'"

That said, I also think it's important to understand that the Beatitudes were not given to us as commands, *but as realities* for the Christian life. They aren't necessarily something we do— rather, they become *who we are* and *how we live* as Christ lives in and through us. I hope this encourages you as you continue through this book. It's really not about you working for God, but God doing his work through you. Notice the wording again: "Blessed are the merciful, for they will be shown mercy." This statement begins Christ's first teaching on how he expects us to treat other people: with mercy.

Years ago, Max Lucado drew a great distinction between grace and mercy via the story of the Prodigal Son. He tweeted, "The difference between mercy and grace? Mercy gave the Prodigal Son a second chance. Grace gave him a feast."[12] This is a really fantastic insight, isn't it? You see, grace is defined as *getting* what you don't deserve, while mercy is defined as *not getting* what you *do* deserve. Mercy gives people second chances.

It's also really important to know that God is not just the distributor of mercy; mercy isn't just what God does, it is *who* God is. God is merciful. Mercy is an attribute of God's character; it flows from his being. God is a God of second chances. And my guess is that right now you might need a second chance—or at least you know someone else who does. Maybe you dropped the ball with your wife this morning . . . Maybe you're struggling with a child who's walked away from Christ . . . Maybe you have a friend who hasn't been a good friend—but wants to reconnect. We all need second chances, and we should all extend second chances.

Let me encourage you to digest the following verses for growth and motivation.

1 Chronicles 21:13 tells us that his mercy is very great. God has endless strengths—including his mercy.

Nehemiah 9:31, NIV, speaks of "your great mercy." We know Nehemiah continually needed and relied upon God's mercy to rebuild the wall.

Luke 1:78 tells us that Christ came because of the tender mercies of our God. God's giving up his son to save us is an act of tender mercy.

Romans 9:16 says that God's election springs from God's mercy. Doctrinally, God's mercy informs his choosing to save people.

Ephesians 2:4 says that God is rich in mercy. God is not cheap with his mercy—he is rich in it.

Hebrews 4:16 tells us that, when we go to Jesus in prayer, we are going to a throne of grace where we can receive mercy and find grace.

According to Titus 3:5, God saved us because of his mercy.

James 5:11 declares that the Lord is full of compassion and mercy.

I also find it fascinating that a major doctrinal theme in the Old Testament speaks of the *mercy seat* in the Holy of Holies. This was the place where God accepted the propitiatory (satisfactory) sacrifice for the sins of the nation of Israel once each year on the Day of Atonement. At the mercy seat, God moved with mercy and compassion towards sinful humanity. In Leviticus 16, he reconciled people to himself by accepting the blood of a goat in their place.

We see that mercy is integral in God's redemption of humanity. Literally, from the time of the fall in Genesis 3, humanity has had *no* way back to God except through the gift of his mercy and grace. With this in mind, it's not at all surprising that the words translated as *mercy* in both the Old and New Testaments are used over 500 times.

For me then, the big idea behind verse 7 is this: Mercy known should translate into mercy shown. Mercy received should become mercy extended. You see, nothing proves that we have received God's mercy more than our own willingness and readiness to dispense God's mercy to others. Again, evaluate yourself here. When someone offends you or sins against you, are you merciful—or judgmental? Are you eager to show mercy or hesitant to show mercy? Is your default mode *getting even*—or *giving someone a second chance*? Be honest!

Now, we do need to tread carefully here because many people have wrongly interpreted and misapplied the meaning of verse 7. Some people say, "Those who are merciful will receive God's mercy." For the record, that is *not* what Jesus is saying! Jesus is not saying that God's mercy towards us *depends* on our extending mercy to others—that is works-based salvation! Many people think they are saved based on what they do instead of on what Christ has done.

Seriously, our being merciful doesn't earn us salvation. It simply *demonstrates* it. In reality, this beatitude presumes you've already received the mercy of God by trusting in God's Son—Jesus.

In the same way, we don't forgive others in order to be forgiven by God. Neither do we extend mercy in order to receive mercy from God. The Bible is super straightforward on this. We are saved by grace alone—through faith in Christ alone. We don't *do* something to be saved because Jesus has already done everything to save us. To really grasp this verse is to understand that God is both the *source of mercy* and our *resource for mercy*.

We don't generate our own mercy—it becomes the overflow of our relationship with Jesus Christ—truly knowing him. As Edmund Clowney put it, "God requires a mercy that cannot be required."[13] We don't manufacture mercy for others—we receive it from God and dispense it to others. Our being merciful to others is simply an outpouring of the mercy of God in our own lives.

I like how Tim Keller said it: "The ministry of mercy is a sacrifice of praise to God's grace!"[14] His point is that, as the merciful person remembers her own sin and God's mercy extended to her—she then willingly extends that mercy to others. Obviously, there are a million ways to demonstrate mercy—because mercy is simply compassion in action and a willingness to give someone a second chance.

We can show mercy in so many ways—by . . .

- forgiving our children when they hurt or offend us,
- demonstrating compassion to the hurting and homeless,
- caring for orphans financially or through adoption,
- giving to meet the needs of those who suffer and struggle,
- alleviating the misery of hungry children and hurting mothers, and
- speaking the gospel of Christ, demonstrating that sharing the gospel is a gesture of mercy.

The point is obvious; if you've received God's mercy, then you must extend it in *any* way you can. If you see a need, then act. Be a person of impact. Be willing to give others a second chance. Be willing to be vulnerable by giving someone mercy.

My favorite illustration of how mercy extended can result in lives impacted comes from one of my favorite novels and movies, *Les Miserables.* The tale takes place during a time of political and social upheaval in France. Jean Valjean, the main character, is a poor tree trimmer who steals a loaf of bread to feed his sister's family. Convicted of theft, he spends 18 years in the slave galleys, rowing the seas in misery. Upon his release, he is hardened, angry, and ready for vengeance. He stays in the home of a priest because no one else will give him lodging.

During his overnight stay, he robs the priest of a silver candlestick and tries to slip out of town in the darkness of night. Later, when apprehended, he is brought back to the priest for identification. The priest looks him dead in the eye and tells the police, that he gave him the candlestick. He then picks up another candlestick and says that he actually gave a pair of them to Valjean, who, in a rush had forgotten the other when he left.

Released by the police and overwhelmed by the priest's mercy, Valjean's life is forever altered. Amazingly, as the recipient of mercy, he refuses to head down the path of vengeance again and literally spends the rest of his life showing mercy to the unfortunate—even to those who had wronged him. I love that story. Mercy changes people.

James and John were both impacted by this beatitude of Jesus. Both actually use the *ministry of mercy* as a test for authentic conversion in believers. For example, John says, "If anyone has the world's goods and sees his brother in need, yet closes his heart against him, how does God's love abide in him? Little children, let us not love in word or talk but in deed and in truth." (1 John 3:17–18).

John's point is that mercy extended authenticates conversion. It reveals we have the love of God in us. It calls us to action—because talk of mercy is cheap and inauthentic.

Likewise, James 2 says that a profession of faith unaccompanied by acts of mercy simply shows that faith to be dead and disingenuous. In verses 14–17, he says, "What good is it, my brothers, if someone says he has faith but does not have works? Can that faith save him? If a brother or sister is poorly clothed and lacking in daily food, and one of you says to them, 'Go in peace, be warmed and filled,' without giving them the things needed for the body, what good is that? So also faith by itself, if it does not have works, is dead." Therefore, real faith is not just something you say (verse 14) . . . real faith is not just something you feel . . . real faith is mercy in action—or it is dead faith.

The kicker for me is James 2:13: "For judgment is without mercy to one who has shown no mercy. Mercy triumphs over judgment." James says judgment without mercy will be shown to anyone who has not been merciful. God judges our lack of mercy. Moreover, in the Proverbs, we see that to ignore the needs of a poor man is to sin against the Lord. So our treatment of the poor and needy is a test of our mercy. Our merciful response to the poor authenticates the genuineness of our faith in God all throughout the Scriptures.

In my opinion, no passage is clearer on this point than Matthew 25:31–46, NIV. Here, Jesus describes his examination of humanity on judgment day. Jesus distinguishes those who have true faith from those who do not by examining their acts of mercy—namely their concern for the poor, homeless, sick, and imprisoned. Jesus drops the hammer when he says, "Whatever you did for one of the least of these brothers and sisters of mine, you did for me." In that way, we see that our mercy towards the least of these is actually a ministry towards Jesus, himself. This is stunning!

This amazing alignment amongst Proverbs, James, John, and Jesus indicates that our acts of mercy towards others are an inevitable outcome, a sign of true faith in us. Here are a few questions to consider: When was the last time you gave someone a second chance? When was the last time you extended a hand of mercy towards the poor, towards someone hurting, homeless, sick, or imprisoned? What individual have you written off over and over again? Show mercy. Extend mercy without judgement, or you'll be shown judgment without mercy from God. The cutthroats do not win in the end.

In closing, the call is really clear: we are to be people who extend mercy instead of withholding it. Let's be people who graciously give people second chances. Let's embrace a merciful lifestyle because mercy triumphs over judgment.

Here's the reality I see: the world is dying for a second chance—and dying to know that God gives second chances. So we need to let everyone near and far know that the heart of God is to save—not condemn. God is a God of second chances.

Ask the Lord to give you the courage and strength to give your mother a second chance—to give your father a second chance—to give your son, your daughter, your friend a second chance. Be merciful because mercy can change someone's life forever!

God, please help me to be merciful to those who have hurt and offended me. Please give me wisdom in treating people mercifully. Thank you for giving me numerous second chances in life. Amen.

CHAPTER 6

BLESSED ARE THE PURE IN HEART

Blessed are the pure in heart, for they shall see God.
MATTHEW 5:8

It probably doesn't come as much of a surprise to you to hear that *purity* is a word greatly prized in the Bible. Think about it. The Word of God repeatedly says that God is holy, Jesus is sinless, and the Holy Spirit convicts us of—and cleanses us of—sin. So it's pretty clear where the triune God stands on the topic of purity. Yet in our society, impurity is wreaking havoc—personally, relationally, politically, and technologically. Culture bombards us with impure pornographic images and thoughts all day—every day.

I'm convinced our culture needs a new vision for purity, and this is the beatitude that will cast the vision to give us the victory we need over impurity. As one commentator said, "Of all the eight beatitudes, none arrests us with a greater sense of sublimity and majesty than this. . . . Like some inaccessible Alpine peak, covered with virgin snow, this conception of the pure heart towers up amid all the great words of this marvelous discourse."[15]

The pure in heart will *see* God!

Think about the awesomeness of that statement for a moment—a chance to *see* the Creator and Sustainer, the All-powerful, Always-present, All-knowing God of the universe. Stunning!

Over the years I've seen—in person—famous athletes, actors, singers, and even a former President of the United States; but to *see God*—is really an unfathomable thought! You may be wondering, "How can I see God when the Scripture repeatedly says that no one can see God and *live*?" Moses desperately wanted to see God. Exodus 33:18–20, 23, NIV, says, "Then Moses said, 'Now show me your glory.'

"And the LORD said, 'I will cause all my goodness to pass in front of you, and I will proclaim my name, the LORD, in your presence. I will have mercy on whom I will have mercy, and I will have compassion on whom I will have compassion. But,' he said, 'you cannot see my face, for no one may see me and live.' . . . 'Then I will remove my hand and you will see my back; but my face must not be seen.'"

Did you read that?

No one can see God and *live*!

To see God's essence and glory is greater than staring directly into the sun—and consider that the sun's light is so bright that it will destroy your eyesight. Shockingly, God's glory is described as infinitely greater, boundlessly brighter, unbelievably more powerful than the sun. 1 Timothy 6:16, NIV, says, "[God] who alone is immortal and who lives in unapproachable light, whom no one has seen or can see. To him be honor and might forever. Amen."

1 John 4:12 states, "No one has ever seen God."

According to the Bible, no one has *ever* seen God because *no one* could handle it *other than Jesus*. So, what is Jesus getting at in this beatitude? Let's break it down. "Blessed are the pure in heart." The Greek word for *pure* is *katharos*. It gives us our English word *catharsis*. If you've had a cathartic experience, it means you've had an emotional cleansing—a releasing of pain, heartache, or baggage. In the Scriptures, *katharos* was also used in numerous other contexts: something free of blemish, spot, or stain; one who is free from corrupt desires and sins; a river whose course was unimpeded; one free of guilt and shame; and an army that has been purged of all the discontented, unwilling, or inefficient soldiers. Obviously, *katharos* is a rich word with powerful images to consider.

Now, the Pharisees would have loved the idea of "blessed are the pure in heart." They put a lot of energy into upholding the stipulations of the ceremonial law found in Leviticus, Chapters 11–15. One of those stipulations stated that if you were to come into contact with someone or something that was unclean, then you were unfit for worship. All of which meant that you had to go through a strenuous purification rite before you were ready to serve God or worship him again.

Somewhere along the way, the Pharisees started playing the *what if* game. They asked, "Well, *what if* you accidentally touched unclean food?" or "What if you accidentally bumped into an unclean Gentile?"

Then what?

This is where the Pharisees got off base and created a misguided extra-biblical religion, embracing their rules but letting go of the Scriptures. They scored an A+ on being outwardly pure, but flunked the inward purity test; all of which tells us that being pure on the surface is not the same as being pure at the center of your being.

Today we see lots of people—both inside and outside the church—striving for moral reformation. However, the grave danger is that our quest for *morality* can actually keep us from genuine Christianity.

John MacArthur pointed out Puritan Thomas Watson's word on the subject. "'Morality can drown a man as fast as a vice' and 'A vessel may sink with gold or with dung.' Though we may be extremely religious and constantly engaged in doing good things, we cannot please God unless our hearts are right with Him."[16]

Watson meant that self-righteous people need to be rescued by Jesus just as much as unrighteous people do. The ultimate danger in self-righteousness, then, is that it usurps the place of the gospel. From that perspective, if I can establish my own right standing before God by who I am or by what I do, then I have no need for the cross of Christ.

Pointing them to the right path, in Matthew 23:25, NIV, Jesus criticized the religious leaders of his day for being content with surface-level cosmetic changes, instead of seeking heart-level (at the core) change. "Woe to you, teachers of the law and Pharisees, you hypocrites! You clean the outside of the cup and dish, but inside they are full of greed and self-indulgence."

The Pharisees spent a lot of time debating on how to keep a kosher kitchen—subsequently creating numerous complex rules along the way. Consider some examples.

- "An *earthen* vessel which is *hollow* becomes unclean only on the inside and not on the outside; and it can be cleansed only by being broken."
- Some earthen vessels "cannot become unclean at all—a flat plate without a rim, an open coal-shovel, a grid-iron with holes in it for roasting grains of wheat."
- "On the other hand, a plate with a rim, or an earthen spice box, or a writing case can become unclean."

- As well, "of vessels made of leather, bone, wood and glass, flat ones do not become unclean; deep ones do. If they are broken, they become clean."[17]

The bottom line is that they got all twisted up over dishes and cups but didn't think twice about cheating or extortion or theft so long as the cookware was externally and ceremonially clean. The obvious application is that keeping up appearances while your private world is in shambles is hypocrisy, which is unacceptable to God. It would be like working out at the gym and sweating for two hours—and then putting on a tuxedo. You might look good on the outside, but you'd smell awful on the inside!

Unfortunately, this ideology is still prevalent in the church world. For a lot of people—as long as you go to church, give a few bucks here and there, volunteer on occasion—then it doesn't matter whether you are dishonest in business, covetous in money matters, cruel to your families, selfish, proud, or arrogant.

But Jesus said otherwise.

He called it hypocrisy. He said, "You clean the outside of the cup and dish, but inside they are full of greed and self-indulgence" (Matthew 23:25, NIV), to which he commanded them in verse 26, "First clean the inside of the cup and dish, and then the outside also will be clean."

Let me explain it this way: We need to be extremely careful not to emphasize outward obedience at the expense of inner renewal. Be especially careful of this with your children. Get to their hearts! Preach the gospel. Our children need Jesus, not the religion of morality to deceive them into thinking they are clean. Remember, our good works don't make us clean. Only the blood of Christ cleanses us from sin.

Obviously then, Christ's point is that purity is far more than dealing with the exterior. Jesus is not talking about cleaning up your act or reforming yourself to become the best version of you.

He is talking about a *heart* transformation.

Clearly, Jesus was not affirming the Pharisaical vision of purity; he was establishing God's vision for purity—a purity that begins at the core of your being.

I'll concede that what makes the Pharisee's approach to purity alluring is that it is quantifiable. I can count the laws, I can keep score, and I can compare myself to others; which makes it easy for me to delude myself into thinking that if I *look* holy to others, I *am* holy. However, the Bible is clear that if the inside—the heart—doesn't change, then ultimately, nothing will change. There can be no *new you* without a *new heart*—and only God can give you a new heart through faith in Christ.

Considering this, the human predicament is clear: We need pure hearts in order to see God, but we can't cleanse ourselves.

Nowhere is this clearer than in the Old Testament. In the law of Moses, every approach to God began with an act of cleansing. Not even the high priest, the only worshiper permitted to enter directly into God's presence, was exempt from this expectation. Moreover, there were also various foods, actions, and conditions that made a person unclean, which prompted subsequent ceremonies for cleansing.

It's important to understand that Old Testament worship was actually built around the concept of a substitute, and the ceremonial cleansing in the law of Moses was appropriated through the shedding of blood. The book of Hebrews says, "In fact, the law requires that nearly everything be cleansed with blood, and without the shedding of blood there is no forgiveness." (Hebrews 9:22, NIV).

However, this system was limited. Even though it was prescribed by God, it couldn't *fully* and *finally* cleanse the believer from sin. Sadly, these ceremonies, as significant as they were, couldn't reach the center from which all thoughts and actions flow. These ceremonies were unable to cleanse the heart. And since they couldn't cleanse the heart, they were also unable to cleanse the conscience. The best they could do is to remind the worshipers of their need to be cleansed over and over again.

In the New Testament, there was also a monumental concern with cleansing, but from a different angle. Hebrews 9:13–14,

NIV, says, "The blood of goats and bulls and the ashes of a heifer sprinkled on those who are ceremonially unclean sanctify them so that they are outwardly clean. How much more, then, will the blood of Christ, who through the eternal Spirit offered himself unblemished to God, cleanse our consciences from acts that lead to death, so that we may serve the living God!" Whereas the Old Testament sacrificial system of bulls and goats could only go so far, the New Testament establishes Christ as the ultimate, once-and-for-all-time sacrifice.

Let's put that in English. Humanity has a problem that only one man can fix—the God-man Jesus. Christ's death on the cross, when applied by faith to our sin, purifies us from *all* unrighteousness and enables us to begin to see God and to see how he works. This is why a person described their conversion to Christ like the lifting of a curtain. There was *no great feeling*: It was a case of *seeing*.

Did you catch that?

Actually, this makes perfect sense. You see, 2 Corinthians 4:4 says, "The god of this age has blinded the minds of unbelievers, so that they cannot see the light of the gospel that displays the glory of Christ, who is the image of God" (NIV). And so, when people are converted to Christ, their blinded spiritual eyes become un-blinded and thus empowered to see the gospel and glory of Christ. Don't miss the connection here. Trusting Christ purifies us, and purity of heart cleanses the eyes of the soul so that God is visible. Spurgeon stated that there is a powerful connection between the heart and the eyes: "If the heart is foul, the eye will be dim."[18]

I am utterly convinced there are two reasons we struggle so much with real transformation. First, people are trying to self-help their way to transformation. But sadly, every self-help strategy is a half-measure that focuses on the exterior, instead of the heart. I hate to break this to you (especially if you've spent a lot of cash in the "self-help section" of Barnes & Noble), but self-help is no help! If you don't believe me, read Proverbs 3:5–6. "Trust in the LORD with all your heart, and do not lean on your own understanding. In all your ways acknowledge him, and he will make straight your paths." Did you see that? Don't lean on yourself! Trust in Christ!

The second reason many people never see God is that it's impossible to see a holy God while embracing an unholy lifestyle. An ungodly, immoral lifestyle impedes spiritual vision. This is why we need to take our sin seriously, as we've already discussed in Chapter 2. Big picture: The Bible says we see God at our conversion—our blinded eyes are un-blinded—and we see God during our sanctification into Christ-likeness as the Spirit convicts us of sin, prompting us to confess our sins! Therefore, those with purified hearts are purified in vision, too; they will see God and see him work.

Interestingly, the Greek word for *see* is *optanomai*. It's where we get the words *optic* and *ophthalmology*, and it means to see physically with the eyes and also to have actual perception and comprehension, to grasp, to attain awareness.

Optanomai is used four times in 1 Corinthians 15:5–8 to describe Jesus' post-resurrection appearances: "He appeared to Cephas, then to the twelve. Then he appeared to more than five hundred brothers at one time, most of whom are still alive, though some have fallen asleep. Then he appeared to James, then to all the apostles. Last of all, as to one untimely born, he appeared also to me."

Optanomai is also repeatedly used to refer to Jesus' second coming. When Jesus returns, I want to see and understand in full the ramifications for my life.

One way you know God is at work inside you is when you begin to understand, to grasp biblical concepts and the truth about who God is! Said another way, when you "get" it and start "seeing" it—God is at work in you.

I absolutely love the simplicity of this beatitude. The pure in heart will see God *for themselves*. This is the promise we can claim! I love that none of us have to settle for a secondhand encounter with God. We don't have to just read about someone else's experience; we can see him for ourselves and experience him ourselves.

In closing, please realize that, according to the Bible, one day some will see God and rejoice—while others will see God and run! Don't miss this—the Bible also describes a clear vision of God in which there is no blessedness. Revelation 6:15–16, NIV, says, "Then the kings of the earth, the princes, the generals, the rich, the mighty, and everyone else, both slave and free, hid in caves and among the rocks of the mountains. They called to the mountains and the rocks, 'Fall on us and hide us from the face of him who sits on the throne and from the wrath of the Lamb!'"

The point Jesus is making is that one day all of humanity will end up face-to-face with God. And in that future moment of monumental consequence, some will want to run from His presence because the ramifications of their rejection of Christ will be perfectly clear. The wrath of God will be upon them. Literally, it will be such a weighty, awesome moment that people will be—think about this—praying for the mountains and the rocks to fall on them, to crush them so they won't have to *see* His face. I hope this sober reality gives you a sense of the awesomeness of seeing God face-to-face without knowing Christ: People will rather be *crushed* by Mt. Everest than to stand *face-to-face* with the God they have rejected!

Fortunately, the great news is that for those whose hearts have been cleansed by the blood of Jesus Christ, there is no greater vision for our lives than *seeing* and *grasping* in some small way who God really is and what God has done. The Bible even says one day our faith will give way to sight! Revelation 22 describes it this way:

> Then the angel showed me the river of the water of life, as clear as crystal, flowing from the throne of God and of the Lamb down the middle of the great street of the city. On each side of the river stood the tree of life, bearing twelve crops of fruit, yielding its fruit every month. And the leaves of the tree are for the healing of the nations. No longer will there be any curse. The throne of God and of the Lamb will be in the city, and his servants will serve him. *They will see his face, and his name will be on their foreheads.* There will be no more night. They will not need the light of a lamp or the light of the sun, for the Lord God will give them light. And they will reign for ever and ever. The angel said to me, . . . "Blessed are those who wash their robes, that they may have the right to the tree of life and may go through the gates into the city."
> —(Revelation 22:1–5, 14, NIV, emphasis added)

Let's not kid ourselves by thinking we can reform our lives by a few good works here and there. Let's humble ourselves and trust in Christ alone to purify us and cleanse us from all sin, thus enabling us to see God and see him work in our world!

God, please help me to see my sin as sin. Please enable me to see you—and you alone—as the only hope of salvation. Give me a passion for purity so I can see you and your work clearly. Amen.

CHAPTER 7

BLESSED ARE THE PEACEMAKERS

Blessed are the peacemakers, for they
will be called children of God.
MATTHEW 5:9, NIV

A lot of occupations in the world today are really danger-ous. Statistically, some of the most perilous jobs include loggers, roofers, construction workers, police officers, and of course, pastors—depends on the church, I guess.

In all seriousness, high on the list of "most hazardous jobs" is fishing on the Alaskan king crabbing boats in the Bering Sea.[19] If you've ever watched *Discovery Channel's Deadliest Catch*, you can attest to the threats of the job. The Bureau of Labor Statistics points to an annual fatality rate of 300 per 100,000 workers. "Over 80% of these deaths are caused by drowning or hypothermia." For some perspective, the fatality rate amongst these fishermen is about 90 times the fatality rate of the average worker.[20]

With that in mind, I want to warn you about another very hazardous job—the Bible calls us to be peacemakers. And no, I am not kidding! Peacemaking is a super-dangerous job because peacemakers engage in high-risk, volatile, inflammatory situations like war on an international scale, fighting amongst family members, sexual abuse incidents, marital conflict, and relational brokenness between brothers and sisters in Christ.

It's important to know that when you *do something,* when you engage, when you get involved, when you step up and step in . . . sometimes it goes well, and sometimes it doesn't.

Charles Forbes tells us that in the fifth century, a monk named Telemachus had been living by himself in the desert, trying to devote himself to God. During that time, he realized that he really couldn't serve God without serving other people. So, he abandoned his life of solitude and traveled to the city of Rome, arriving just in time to watch a victory celebration in which Gothic prisoners were being forced to battle one another to the death as gladiators. Ironically, during that time, Rome considered itself a "Christian" city, yet the churches *emptied* to see this bloody spectacle.

When the monk saw the crowd of 80,000 roaring for the blood of the two gladiators as they fought each other, he was horrified. He was so outraged that he charged into the arena and placed himself between the two warring gladiators, pleading with them to stop the conflict. Furious over the delay in their entertainment, the spectators stoned Telemachus to death.

Three days later, the emperor declared him a martyr and did away with gladiatorial contests altogether.[21]

Telemachus had achieved his goal as a peacemaker, yet in the process, he lost his life. Obviously, I'm giving you an extreme example, but peacemaking can be dangerous business. Honestly, the biggest reason we know it is hazardous to be a peacemaker is that the greatest peacemaker who *ever* lived was nailed to a tree. It shouldn't be lost on anyone that Jesus preached the gospel of peace and died in an act of cruel violence. That's right. Jesus is the greatest peacemaker in history—making peace between sinful humanity and holy God—and he was crucified.

So, when we read Jesus' words, "Blessed are the peacemakers for they will be called sons of God," I'd simply say (in the peacemaking process) don't forget what happened to the Son of God.

There is also something glorious about being a peacemaker; so I don't want to scare you, but rather help you establish the right level of expectation. Spurgeon said, "This is the seventh of the beatitudes: and seven was the number of perfection among the Hebrews. It may be that the Savior placed the peacemaker seventh upon the list because he most nearly approaches the perfect man in Christ Jesus."[22] Jesus personified the perfect peace of God.

Let's dig into this verse. The Greek word for *peacemaker* is *eirene-poieo*. It's a word that means making peace, instead of war. The related Hebrew word is *shalom*. Just so you'll know, *peace* in the Bible is a really broad term related to health, prosperity, harmony, and wholeness. It's not just a tranquil, meditative state of mind—it is an intentional way of living.

The most prolific author in the New Testament, Paul, wrote extensively about peace. The irony behind this is that he didn't write about peace from a luxurious bed-and-breakfast villa in Ephesus. Most of his letters came from a dirty prison, where the outcome of his life hung in the balance. Clearly, Paul wants us to think about peace differently! From Paul's life, you see that he didn't need circumstances to rightly align in order to have peace. He only needed Jesus to have peace. His message on peace was always consistent: peace shouldn't be contingent upon anything but Christ.

Now this is a counter-cultural way to think—it really is—but, to put it into today's terms, Paul is essentially saying that

- Peace should never be based on whether or not the sun shines.
- Peace should never be based on whether or not he calls you back.
- Peace should never be based on whether or not the check comes in.
- Peace should never be based on whether or not the stock market fluctuates.

- Peace should never be based on whether or not you get a raise or a promotion.
- Peace should never be based on whether or not you make the team.
- Peace should never depend on your circumstances.

Does any of this strike a chord? Finding peace only when things are going your way will lead to fluctuating joy; but finding peace in Christ is constant because Jesus is the same yesterday, today and forever!

It's one thing to experience the peace of God personally and quite another to be a peacemaker culturally. Let's talk about being a peacemaker. First, the word *make* in the term *peacemakers* is really important for us to understand because it tells us that peace must be *made*; peace never just happens by chance. Peacemakers intentionally bring combatants to the table and give them a reason to put down their weapons. Their goal is to *make* peace—to make peace happen.

As well, pay attention to the fact that Jesus doesn't bless those who have a *peaceful disposition*, as good as that might be. He doesn't say, "Blessed are those who are *peaceful*." The focus here is not on the *personality*, but on the *action* of the person Jesus describes. Those who are blessed are those who *make* peace.

There's a huge difference between minding your own business and being a peacemaker. A peacemaker knows that dealing with the conflict *is* his or her business. Clearly, peacemaking is not a passive characteristic. In actuality, the language Jesus uses is dynamic; thus, a peacemaker is one who leans into the situation, confronts it head on, and is in turn blessed by God!

Please know I'm not saying that being a peacemaker is just about having amazing people skills. Peacemaking is a work of grace, for sure. Said another way, we don't begin with peace as a *task*, we start with peace as a *gift*, because that's how peace came to us—as a gift.

Why is that important?

Well, it would be really easy for you to read these words about peacemaking and simply think that being a peacemaker is all about becoming a skilled negotiator or a skilled diplomat able to broker a cease-fire between people. While this is a part of it; again, we don't begin with peace as a task. We start with peace as a gift. Peace is what God gives and what he brings! We don't make or give or bring peace. God does.

From a biblical perspective, then, the foundational reason there is no lasting peace in the world is that a civil war rages within the heart of man. This war in the heart of man inhibits peace *in the world*. Put another way, if peace doesn't exist *in the hearts of people*, peace will never permeate the culture in which we live. Actually, the Bible clearly says that humanity has been at war with God since Genesis 3! Over in the New Testament, Paul describes our war with God in vivid terms in each of these passages:

> For although they knew God, they neither glorified him as God nor gave thanks to him, but their thinking became futile and their foolish hearts were darkened.
> —Romans 1:21, NIV

> They exchanged the truth about God for a lie, and worshiped and served created things rather than the Creator—who is forever praised. Amen.
> —Romans 1:25, NIV

As it is written:

> "There is no one righteous, not even one;
>   there is no one who understands;
>   *there is no one who seeks God.*
> *All have turned away,*
>   they have together become worthless;
> *there is no one who does good,*
>   not even one."

"Their throats are open graves;
   their tongues practice deceit."
"The poison of vipers is on their lips."
   "Their mouths are full of cursing and bitterness."
"Their feet are swift to shed blood;
   ruin and misery mark their ways,
and *the way of peace they do not know.*"
   "*There is no fear of God before their eyes.*"
—Romans 3:10–18, NIV, emphasis added

Notice the depth of humanity's rebellion in these passages
of Scripture:

- "There is no one who seeks God."
- "All have turned away."
- "There is no one who does good."
- "The way of peace they do not know."
- "There is no fear of God before their eyes."

And so if you don't have God's peace within you, you
cannot bring God's peace to others, locally, nationally, or
internationally.

Therefore, you have to ask yourself, "Am I at peace with God?
Do I really understand where true peace comes from?"

The Bible is clear that God's peace plan is the gospel. Every human on the face of the planet can be saved only by *grace* alone through *faith* alone in *Christ alone*! Once we experience, then, the peace of God through Christ—we are to share that plan with *everyone who has a pulse.*

One commentator said it like this: "Blessed are those who announce to sinful men the fact that a Savior has come."[23] Paul summed up our job description as Christians in a similar way. "Therefore, if anyone is in Christ, the new creation has come: The old has gone, the new is here! All this is from God, who reconciled us to himself through Christ and gave us the ministry of reconciliation: that God was reconciling the world to himself in Christ, not counting people's sins against them. And he has committed to us the message of reconciliation. We are therefore Christ's ambassadors, as though God were making his appeal through us. We implore you on Christ's behalf: Be reconciled to God." (2 Corinthians 5:17–20, NIV). Christ has come to bring peace between God and man! And once you become a new creation, you are then called to a new life direction: Christ's ambassador. Therefore, after the war in your own soul has ended by your trusting in Jesus Christ, your immediate task is to spread God's peace plan to everyone else still at war with God. In that sense, evangelism is ultimately a form of peacemaking!

Additionally, please understand that being a peacemaker also means that we intervene by bringing the peace of God where there is conflict between people—especially God's people. One problem is that most people are scared of conflict. We avoid conflict just as we avoid going outside when it's minus 40 degrees. We dodge confrontational, intense conversations. Years ago I read the book *Fierce Conversations* by Susan Scott. The premise of Scott's book is that our lives succeed or fail one conversation at a time. She says that avoiding tough conversations means we don't value the relationship like we should. As a result, nothing much happens when our greatest value is conflict avoidance. Let me tell you this: avoiding conflict is unacceptable for God's people. We are to seek peace, care about peace, make peace. We are peacemakers because we are people lovers.

As you well know, we live in a divide-and-conquer world filled with war, unhealthy divisive political discourse, misunderstanding, bitterness, betrayal, anger, slander, lying, hatred, and bloodshed. On every level, there are ruined marriages, fragmented friendships, estranged children, neighbors who won't speak, commuters who drive in a rage, bosses who don't trust their workers, and workers who cheat their bosses. There is not much peace in the world today. Watch the news. We have ethnic groups at war, nations in arms, protests, movements, so many armies, so many bombs, and so much killing.

It is into this chaotic, strife-filled, war-torn world that Christ-followers are called to go as peacemakers. It's into this world that Christians are called to reconcile, intervene, listen, umpire, resolve, and mediate. We are called to do what we can to stop the bloodshed and end the violence by bringing God's *shalom*—his gracious peace—to the world. We are to begin at home and then fan out to the whole wide world. It's a big order, and you might wonder how you could even start to do it.

The truth is that Telemachus had an arena, and so do *you!* Maybe it means that you make a call, send an email, write a letter, run for office, make a meal, pay a debt, set up a meeting, see a friend, entreat an enemy, or preach the gospel of peace. Whatever it is—do something.

Whatever your *something* might be, remember what the last half of Matthew 5:9, NIV, tells us. "Blessed are the peacemakers, for they shall be called sons of God." In the Scriptures, this designation as "sons" is often used in a descriptive sense. To call someone a son was to say that there was a likeness, usually reflected in behavior.

With that in mind, let's answer an important question: why are peacemakers blessed? They are blessed, not as a payment for their efforts—as good as they may be—but because of their position, because of what peacemaking says about them. Peacemakers have a family resemblance to their brother Jesus Christ.

Their actions mark their identity as sons and daughters of God. And so our peacemaking is merely an extension of Christ's work in the world.

Knowing this, let's stop living in fear. Let's stop avoiding conflict and tense, difficult situations. Let's deal with conflict instead of running from it. Let's take our personal peace with God into a world in desperate need of the peace of God. It might feel like an uncomfortable job—even a dangerous one—but Jesus is our model; and he has given us the greatest peace plan in the world: the gospel of Jesus Christ!

God, help me to find my peace in the person of Christ alone. Help me to genuinely experience that peace so I can take the gospel boldly into the world. Today help me to do what I can to advance the cause of peace in my family, my community, and the world. Amen.

CHAPTER 8

BLESSED ARE THOSE WHO ARE PERSECUTED BECAUSE OF RIGHTEOUSNESS

Blessed are those who are persecuted because of
righteousness, for theirs is the kingdom of heaven.
MATTHEW 5:10, NIV

We've covered a lot of ground in this book. We've examined how Jesus describes the blessed life: men and women who are poor in spirit and mourn over their sin. They're the ones who live by God's standards, living lives of meekness and longing for God's righteousness in our culture. They regularly show mercy to others. These believers are pure in heart and seek peace between God and man. You might assume that those who embrace Christ's vision for the blessed life would be accepted, applauded, and even celebrated by the world!

But that is rarely the case.

Christ's last beatitude prophetically tells us that the end game for living out the Beatitudes is not a parade thrown on your behalf, but rather a persecution for your righteous living. "Blessed are those who are persecuted because of righteousness, for theirs is the kingdom of heaven. Blessed are you when people insult you, persecute you and falsely say all kinds of evil against you because of me. Rejoice and be glad, because great is your reward in heaven, for in the same way they persecuted the prophets who were before you" (Matthew 5:10–12, NIV).

The word *persecute* means to pursue as an enemy. It means to chase, harass, vex, and pressure. In the New Testament, Saul—before he became Paul—persecuted Christians. He hunted them down and dragged them out of their homes, harassing and eventually murdering many for their faith in Christ. So, persecution can denote a violent physical attack or a personal attack with words in the form of slander, insults, hatred, or ostracism. Persecution obviously comes in varying degrees. Now—this is so important—Jesus says the *cause* of persecution is *righteousness*.

For the record, there is no blessing in store for people who are persecuted because they are obnoxious knuckleheads, offensive rubes, or overzealous Pharisees; so make sure you don't bring unnecessary persecution upon yourself—this does not please your Father in Heaven! Remember, Jesus is asserting here that a righteous life leads to persecution. A righteous life includes being right with God and people and longing for righteousness to reign in our culture.

Notice too that the blessing in store for those persecuted for the sake of righteousness is—quite amazingly—the kingdom of heaven. The term *kingdom* refers to the territory or people over whom a king rules. By definition, then, this kingdom is the rule and reign of Jesus the King. So, to belong to the kingdom of heaven is to belong to the King. And those who are *in Christ* eagerly await his return and the establishment of his literal earthly kingdom.

As well, notice that Jesus bookends the Beatitudes with the reward of the kingdom of heaven. "Blessed are the poor in spirit, for theirs is the kingdom of heaven. . . . Blessed are those who are persecuted because of righteousness, for theirs is the kingdom of heaven" (Matthew 5:3, 10, NIV). This highlights that Jesus Christ and the kingdom of heaven are our greatest rewards and blessings!

Now I find it interesting that verse 10 is the only beatitude of the eight with some commentary and explanation. You see, verses 11–12 actually elucidate verse 10 for us. "Blessed are you when people insult you, persecute you and falsely say all kinds of evil against you because of me. Rejoice and be glad, because great is your reward in heaven, for in the same way they persecuted the prophets who were before you" (Matthew 5:11–12, NIV). The interpretive progression of verses 10–12 goes like this: my righteous living fuels the world's persecution. God then blesses my loyalty to him (amidst persecution) by giving me joy and the promise of an ultimate reward, which inspires my continued righteousness.

And on and on it goes!

I love verse 10 because it shows us that the joy and blessing of God are more powerful and lasting than the persecution of man. In that sense, persecution does not stop me; instead, God's blessings inspire me to live the righteous Christian life!

In addition, check out that Jesus actually gives us two reasons to "rejoice and be glad" for persecution—first, because you are like the prophets. Spurgeon said, "You are in the true prophetic succession if you cheerfully bear reproach of this kind for Christ's sake—you prove that you have the stamp and seal of those who are in the service of God!"[24] And the second reason? Your reward in heaven is great. If it bothers you to think of rewards, realize that a reward is a gift of God's grace, not something earned. It is not a compensation for work done, but rather a gift which far exceeds services rendered. Please understand that the concept of rewards is neither selfish nor unspiritual. There is a reward in store for those who are persecuted for their commitment to Jesus Christ!

In our culture today, every Christian needs to grasp the reality of persecution, insults, and rejection in order to avoid being disillusioned in the Christian life. 2 Timothy 3:12, NIV, says, "In fact, everyone who wants to live a godly life in Christ Jesus will be persecuted."

Let's just reread that for a moment: "In fact, everyone who wants to live a godly life in Christ Jesus will be persecuted."

It is so important for Christians—particularly for those who are new in the faith—to grasp early on the reality of persecution so they don't become disillusioned or discouraged when they are unexpectedly blindsided by harsh words, ridicule, rejection—or even physical harm.

Please take this to heart: If you are in Christ, persecution is normal. It is par for the course. In the church today, most people tend to think persecution is extreme and abnormal. Yet, the New Testament says otherwise. It clearly declares that the only abnormality is when persecution is absent from our walk with Christ. It's absurd to think that suffering and persecution have no place in the life of a faithful Christ-follower when the founder of the movement—Jesus himself—ended up nailed to a tree. Besides, Jesus told us time and time again to expect it. He said, "If the world hates you, keep in mind that it hated me first. If you belonged to the world, it would love you as its own. As it is, you do not belong to the world, but I have chosen you out of the world. That is why the world hates you. Remember what I told you: 'A servant is not greater than his master.' If they persecuted me, they will persecute you also" (John 15:18–20, NIV).

So, it should not come as a surprise if an unbelieving spouse derides your faith, a university professor demeans your passion for Christ, or a government official throws you in prison.

Take heart. What Jesus said would happen . . . did! And great is your reward in heaven!

It comes down to this: every Christian needs to understand that the goal of Christianity is not to be a nice, popular person who *never* offends anybody. As a matter of fact, Jesus said in Luke 6:26, "Woe to you when everyone speaks well of you, for that is how their ancestors treated the false prophets" (NIV). This verse haunts me because I can easily get caught up in wanting everyone to speak well of me, wanting to be a nice, popular Christian person who never offends anybody. Yet, as Alexander MacLaren said, "Antagonism is inevitable between a true Christian and the world. . . . A true Christian ought to be a standing rebuke to the world, an incarnate conscience!"[25]

Here's the truth: Christians are not *a little* different from the world—they are *altogether* different! With that in mind, let me share a few thoughts about persecution to encourage your faith. If anyone tells you that being a Christ-follower is easy, they are lying. It's not easy. Grace is free—but following Christ demands your whole life—not just one hour on Sunday, but your entire life. And remember, blessing is not found in easiness—it is found through perseverance.

See what Romans 5:3–4 says about suffering. "We rejoice in our sufferings, knowing that suffering produces endurance, and endurance produces character, and character produces hope." Paul says suffering produces perseverance, character, and hope. We can't learn to persevere unless we have to persevere *through* something. We can't develop character unless something *tests* our character. We can't learn to hope unless something better exists for which we *can* hope. Suffering, then, provides the opportunity for perseverance, character, and hope.

If anyone ever tells you that being a follower of Christ is the hip, trendy, mainstream thing to do, they are lying. True Christians are in the minority—always have been and always will be. Following Jesus isn't going to make you popular—nor should it.

If anyone ever tells you that being a follower of Jesus will solve all of your problems, they are lying. In reality, receiving Jesus Christ solves our greatest problem—being separated from God because of sin—but it also guarantees an entirely new set of problems, called *trials*, which Jesus uses to develop our faith. It also opens us up to temptations and persecution from the enemy.

If anyone ever tells you that becoming a follower of Jesus will be a decision everyone close to you will get behind and support, they are lying. Jesus explained it well when he said, "For I have come to set a man against his father, and a daughter against her mother, and a daughter-in-law against her mother-in-law. And a person's enemies will be those of his own household" (Matthew 10:35–36).

If anyone ever tells you that sowing a financial seed will guarantee you a cash harvest, they are lying. As a matter of fact, if you give because it pays—it won't pay! God is not a divine slot machine that we play—He is the God of the universe whom we worship!

You need to know—if you don't already—that righteous living is not valued or celebrated in our culture today. Righteous living will generate persecution. When Jesus says, "Woe to you when all men speak well of you," he means that, if you have never experienced suffering for the sake of righteousness, then you should examine your walk with Jesus Christ; maybe your righteousness isn't quite right.

And so, Mom and Dad, are you raising politically correct Christians or radically focused disciples? Are you mentoring Spirit-empowered, game-changing Christians who live and stand for righteousness—or for something else?

From where I sit, the church seems full of maddeningly bland, generic, culturally accommodating Christians who work harder to *fit in* than to *stand out*. Please know this: not everyone will like you because of the Christ in you! With that understanding, every Christian needs to embrace that the Christian life doesn't get easier; but it does get better.

How so? Well, history tells us Jesus' closest followers were executed. James was beheaded and Phillip crucified. Matthew was slain by the sword. James was stoned to death, while Matthias was stoned, then beheaded. Andrew was crucified and left hanging on the cross for three days—and Peter was crucified upside down. Paul was beheaded by Nero in Rome. Jude was also crucified, and Bartholomew was beaten to death with clubs. Thomas was speared to death. And Simon the Zealot? He was crucified too. Stephen was stoned to death. Finally, John the Baptist was beheaded. Life didn't get easier for these guys; but let me tell you, *it got better*. Great is their reward in heaven.

Do you remember that Jesus mentioned the persecuted prophets in Matthew 5:12? Well, Hebrews 11:32–40 says,

And what more shall I say? I do not have time to tell about Gideon, Barak, Samson and Jephthah, about David and Samuel and the prophets, who through faith conquered kingdoms, administered justice, and gained what was promised; who shut the mouths of lions, quenched the fury of the flames, and escaped the edge of the sword; whose weakness was turned to strength; and who became powerful in battle and routed foreign armies. Women received back their dead, raised to life again. There were others who were tortured, refusing to be released so that they might gain an even better resurrection.

[It doesn't get easier; but it does get better.]

Some faced jeers and flogging, and even chains and imprisonment. They were put to death by stoning; they were sawed in two; they were killed by the sword. They went about in sheepskins and goatskins, destitute, persecuted and mistreated—the world was not worthy of them. They wandered in deserts and mountains, living in caves and in holes in the ground.

These were all commended for their faith, yet none of them received what had been promised, since God had planned something better for us so that only together with us would they be made perfect (NIV).

Notice in verses 35–39, not one of them received what was promised. In this life, they never got what they were looking for—even though they were faithful. The text says they didn't get a reward here on earth. You need to know that you might do exactly what God calls you to do—and still not get what you expect. But that's not the end of the world because so many of us expect the wrong things anyway. We expect a worldly reward for spiritual faithfulness, but God doesn't want us to settle for that. He has so much more to offer us than the world does!

Therefore, don't miss that the key to this is right in the middle of that last paragraph: "The world was not worthy of them" (verse 38). This is so instructive—you see, the author of Hebrews is basically saying these saints of old were so faithful to God that the world had nothing to offer them. They literally *couldn't* receive their reward in this world, because there was nothing in this world that could satisfy them.

Think of it like this: you can't receive blessings from this world if the world is not good enough for you. If you long for heaven, nothing on earth will do. If your passion is for Jesus Christ, nothing the world offers will even come close.

Hebrews 11:40 actually says that God had *something better* planned for us who are in Christ. And that *something better*—a better life and a better future—should keep us inspired to endure the persecution that accompanies the righteous life that honors our great God!

In closing, from the Beatitudes we learn that the blessed life *no one really wants* is actually the *best* life of all!

John Piper, in talking about the presence of Christ and eternal life in heaven, wrote "There's nobody in this room who could offer me anything better. In fact, there's no one in this room or in this world who can even conceive of anything better than fullness of joy and pleasures at his right hand forever. Full. There's nothing fuller than full and there's nothing longer than forever."[26]

This is our future. This is our inheritance. And it is—and it will be—the best and most blessed life ever!

It's the *best life* because Jesus is in it, Jesus is in charge of it, and Jesus is a better way of living. His presence and his kingdom are his greatest gifts to us!

Can we now broaden our understanding of blessing from Chapter 1? How about a new list that embraces both:

- Protection *and* Persecution
- Success *and* Suffering
- Getting Invited *and* Getting Insulted
- Bigger *and* Smaller
- Health *and* Pain
- More *and* Less
- Now *and* Later

Please take some time to reflect on what the Beatitudes really say about blessing—they are counterintuitive to what we know. And please don't allow a focus on the prosperity gospel to creep in and take over your life. The Bible says that knowing God makes us rich in every way and that not knowing God makes us poor—in spite of our wealth.

Finally, the Beatitudes remind us that who Jesus is and what he has offered us through his death and resurrection is the greatest blessing of all.

So what are you going to do?

Are you going to take Jesus at his word?

The choice is yours. Choose wisely.

The truth is the Blessed Life (that no one really wants) is actually where the Blessed Life is truly found.

God, please give me the courage to live righteously. Help me to have the wisdom and strength to endure any form of persecution that comes from following you. Help me to be willing to stand out and stand up for the person of Christ and his purposes in the world. Help me to embrace the blessed life of the Beatitudes. Amen.

Endnotes

1   Philip Yancey, *What's So Amazing About Grace?* (Grand Rapids, MI: Zondervan, 1997), 71.

2   Jonathan T. Pennington, *The Sermon on the Mount and Human Flourishing: A Theological Commentary* (Grand Rapids, MI: Baker Academic, 2017), 42.

3   John Stott, *Essential Living: The Sermon on the Mount* (Downers Grove, IL: InterVarsity Press, 1988), 33.

4   R. Kent Hughes, *The Sermon on the Mount: The Message of the Kingdom* (Wheaton, IL: Crossway Books, 2001), 22.

5   Thomas Watson, *The Beatitudes: An Exposition of Matthew 5:1–12* (Carlisle, PA: The Banner of Truth Trust, 1994), 64.

6   John MacArthur, *The MacArthur New Testament Commentary* (Chicago: Moody Publishers, 1985), 168–70.

7   David Martyn Lloyd-Jones, *Studies in the Sermon on the Mount* (Grand Rapids, MI: Wm. B. Eerdmans Publishing, 1976), 58.

8   R. Kent Hughes, 38.

9   David Martyn Lloyd-Jones, 62.

10 Charles H. Spurgeon, *The Treasury of David* (Peabody, MA: Hendrickson Publishers, 1990), 173.

11 A.W. Tozer, *The Size of the Soul: Principles of Revival and Spiritual Growth* (Chicago: Moody Publishers, 2018), 12.

12 Max Lucado, Twitter, January 17, 2011, https://twitter.com/maxlucado/status /27022300356284416?lang=en.

13 Tim Keller, *Gospel in Life Study Guide: Grace Changes Everything* (Grand Rapids, MI: Zondervan, 2013), 109.

14 Keller, 110.

15 *Sermon Outlines for a New Series of Gospel Lessons*, (St. Louis, MO: Concordia Publishing House, 1914), 464.

16 MacArthur, 205.

17 William Barclay, *The New Daily Study Bible: The Gospel of Matthew, Volume 2*, (Louisville, KY: Westminster John Knox Press, 2001), 344–345.

18 Charles Spurgeon, *NCV, The Devotional Bible: Experiencing The Heart of Jesus*, (Nashville, TN: Thomas Nelson, 2004), 142.

19 Les Christie, "America's most dangerous jobs," *CNN Money*, Published October 13, 2003, Accessed July 8, 2018, http://money.cnn.com/2003/10/13/pf/dangerousjobs/index.htm.

20 "Alaskan king crab fishing," *Wikipedia*, Accessed July 8, 2018, https://en.wikipedia.org /wiki/Alaskan_king_crab_fishing#Danger.

21 Charles Forbes Comte de Montalembert, *The Monks of the West: From St. Benedict to St. Bernard* (Patrick-Donahoe, 1872), 217.

22 Charles Spurgeon, *Morning & Evening.* (Peabody, MA: Hendrickson Publishers, 1991), 155.

23 J. Dwight Pentecost, *Design for Living: Lessons on Holiness from the Sermon on the Mount*, (Grand Rapids, MI: Kregel Publishing, 1999), 63.

24 "The Beatitudes," *Christian Classics Ethereal Library*, Accessed July 8, 2018, https://www.ccel.org/ccel/spurgeon/sermons55.xxxi.html.

25 Alexander MacLaren, *Expositions of Holy Scripture—Ezekiel, Daniel, and the Minor Prophets. St. Matthew Chapters I to VIII* (Filiquarian Publishing, LLC. / Qontro, 2010), 281.

26 John Piper, "The Cost of Love in the Call to the Nations" (sermon, Liberty University Convocation, Liberty University, Lynchburg, VA, Sep 16, 2013).